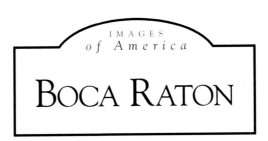

IMAGES
of America

BOCA RATON

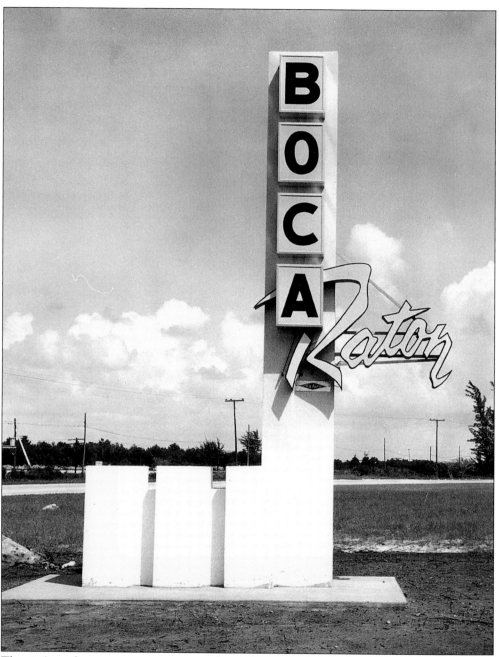

The city's southern entrance sign once welcomed visitors who entered from Broward County.

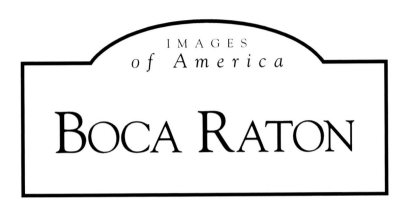

IMAGES
of America

BOCA RATON

Cynthia Thuma

ARCADIA
PUBLISHING

Published by Arcadia Publishing
Charleston, South Carolina

Printed in The United States of America

Library of Congress Catalog Card Number: 2003111352

For all general information contact Arcadia Publishing at:
Telephone 843-853-2070
Fax 843-853-0044
E-mail sales@arcadiapublishing.com
For customer service and orders:
Toll-Free 1-888-313-2665

Visit us on the Internet at www.arcadiapublishing.com

To Ann Romer, the muse and my first guide to Boca Raton.

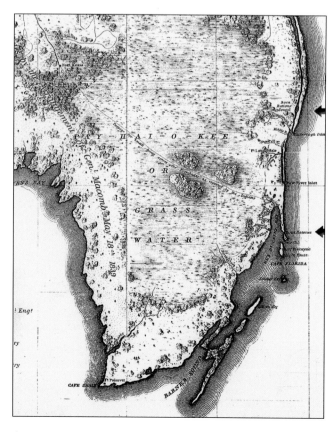

The 1839 map of southern Florida shows two Boca Ratons. The top arrow shows the current one, and the lower arrow shows its original site, at what is now Indian Creek in Miami-Dade County.

CONTENTS

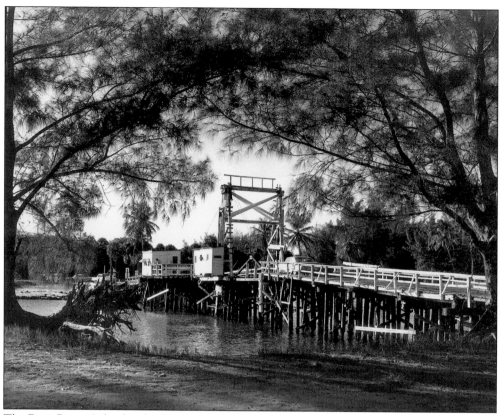

The Boca Raton Inlet drawbridge was a welcoming sight to boaters entering Lake Boca Raton.

ACKNOWLEDGMENTS

First and foremost, my appreciation goes to Mary Csar, the executive director of the Boca Raton Historical Society and to Susan Gillis, its brilliant, talented archivist. Joining them are a small brigade of local experts who helped track down and verify facts to help ensure the accuracy of this book. They are Wendy Kuhlberg, Pat Jakubek, Arlene Owens, and Linda Jackson.

Ginger Pedersen, daughter of Jack Pedersen, and Shirley and George Schneider, daughter and son-in-law of John P. Pedersen, were enormously helpful in teaching me about Africa-U.S.A., an attraction I'd had the pleasure of visiting early in my youth.

Other kind folks who were important to the creation of this book include longtime friends Cindy Newnam and Carlos Barroso, of St. Andrew's School; Fr. Guy Fiano, of Pope John Paul II High School; Katrina McCormack, of Florida Atlantic University; Ruth Tennies, of Boca Raton Christian School; and Neil Evangelista, public information officer for the city of Boca Raton.

INTRODUCTION

Anyone who has taken a Spanish class in high school or college probably knows that "boca" means "mouth" and "raton" means "mouse," but contrary to conventional wisdom, Boca Raton does not mean "mouse mouth." A more likely explanation is that it is a term for an inlet, because it serves as the mouth of a waterway, and Boca Raton indeed has an inlet of its own. The term "raton" can also be used to denote a reluctant or cowardly thief. Romantic legends and tall tales spread by early developers suggested that the calm, relatively shallow waters of Lake Boca Raton provided a haven for pirates and mariners hoping to wait out inclement weather.

Many years ago, there were two similarly named places in southeastern Florida. An 1839 map (on page 4) shows Boca Ratone Inlet located on Biscayne Bay (top arrow) and Boca Ratione Sound where today's Lake Boca Raton is (bottom arrow). The land around the lake was called Rio Seco, or "dry river." While the Palm Beach County city's name stuck, the Miami-Dade County site's did not. That area is now called Indian Creek.

Nowadays, visitors tend to pronounce Boca Raton's name as Boca Rah-tawn. In its early years, the city was called Boca Ratone, which is how the name is properly pronounced—Rah-tone—but around the mid-1920s, the "e" was dropped.

Following a unique and occasionally serpentine course, from an agricultural oasis to a tourist mecca and a silicon beach, Boca Raton has today become a city of education and commerce, a world-class tourist destination, and a wonderful place for families to grow, learn, and play together. It also is an excellent place to enjoy one's sunset years.

This book is not a formal recitation of the city's history; there already are several excellent books that do a superb job of it. The 180-plus images selected for this book are an attempt to show the city, its people, its institutions, and its growth through a variety of people's eyes. Boca Raton has always been about doers and dreamers, entrepreneurs and philanthropists, movers and shakers, and this book touches on them as well as others who normally do not appear in history texts: good neighbors, public and community servants, and hard-working citizens. This book mixes images of them with postcards, illustrations, a few maps, and even some advertisements. Think of this book of images as "history lite" perhaps, but consider each of the faces you see as threads in the fabric that bind this community together. This book is no dry recitation of events past. It offers a chance to weigh the words, look at the images, and enjoy Boca Raton's past in a different way.

The events that are chronicled here hold important lessons for the present and future. South Florida's history is neither as long or storied as other parts of our nation, and many of the communities here are just beginning to discover the need to preserve artifacts and documents of their history, but not so for Boca Raton. The city has an admirable track record and has achieved national recognition for its dedication to historic preservation. Through the dedicated efforts of the Boca Raton Historical Society, this is a community that embraces its history and has made a sustained effort to preserve it as a learning tool.

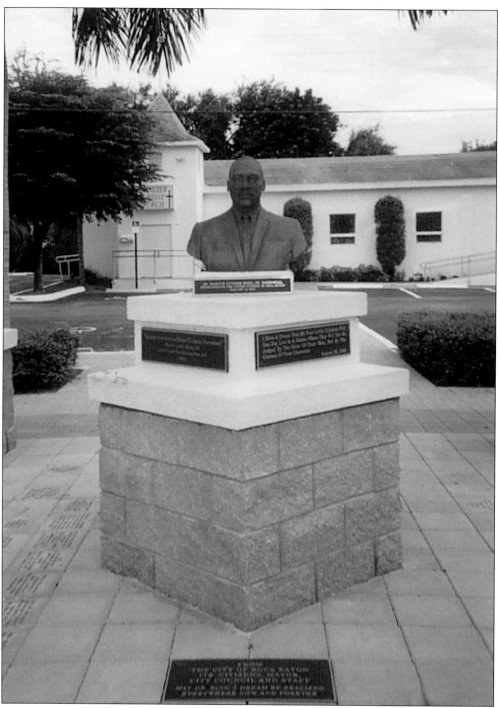

The Dr. Martin Luther King Jr. Memorial was dedicated in January 2001. It sits along Glades Road, right in front of the Ebenezer Baptist Church.

One

IN THE BEGINNING
1895–1909

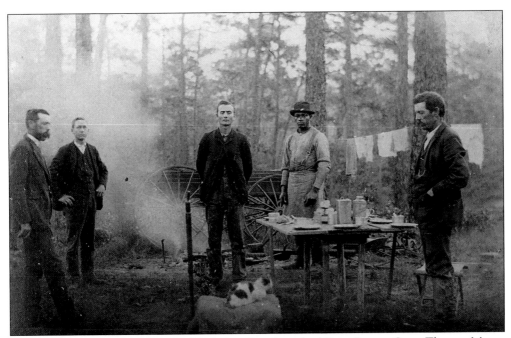

In 1895, the year Henry Morrison Flagler's railroad reached Boca Raton, Capt. Thomas Moore Rickards did, too, though Rickards arrived a bit ahead of Flagler's iron horse. An Ohio-born civil engineer and surveyor, Rickards had worked his way down the peninsula, surveying parcels for the state. Rickards (far right), his brother (far left), and their work crew traveled by wagon and set up camps along the way.

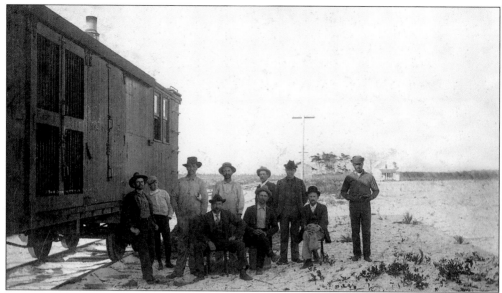

Rickards (third from the right) bought 50 acres along Lake Boca Raton, which he called the Black Cat Plantation. Florida's climate was far more hospitable than Missouri's, where he had been living, and he decided to transplant his wife Lizzy and their five children. He was especially fond of the area on the northern and western shores of Lake Boca Raton, and it was there he decided to plant his own roots. He became the community's first settler. After the railroad arrived, Rickards became Flagler's local agent for the Model Land Company.

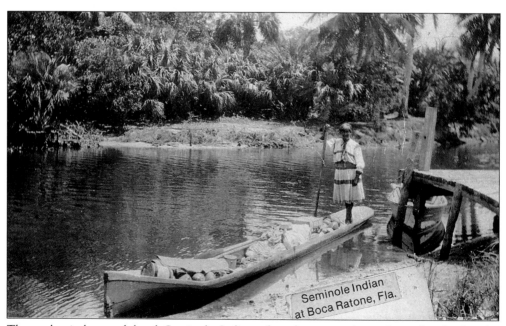

Seminole Indian at Boca Ratone, Fla.

The early settlers and local Seminole Indians forged strong relationships that both sides found beneficial. The Seminoles brought locally grown foods, animal pelts, and other items for barter.

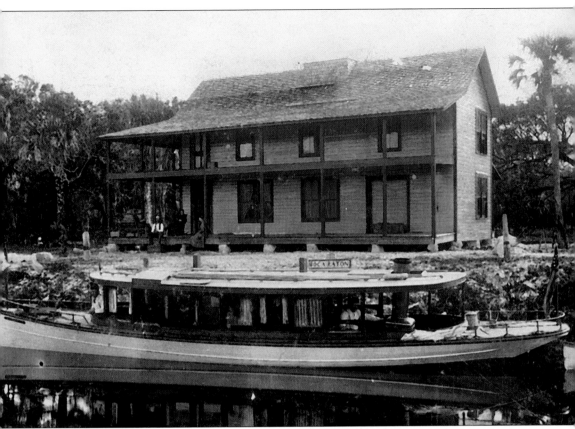

The vessel *Kathleen* plied the waters of southeastern Florida in the mid-1890s, bringing freight, mail, and passengers to stops—such as the Rickards home—along the way. The Rickards home overlooked the Florida East Coast Canal (now the Intracoastal Waterway) south of the current Palmetto Park Road Bridge. In 1902, George Ashley Long and his family arrived in Boca Raton. A friend of Rickards, Boston-born and Harvard-educated Long also worked as a civil engineer. Rickards sold his house to him. By 1906, the hard, harsh life in South Florida had disillusioned Rickards, who moved his family to North Carolina.

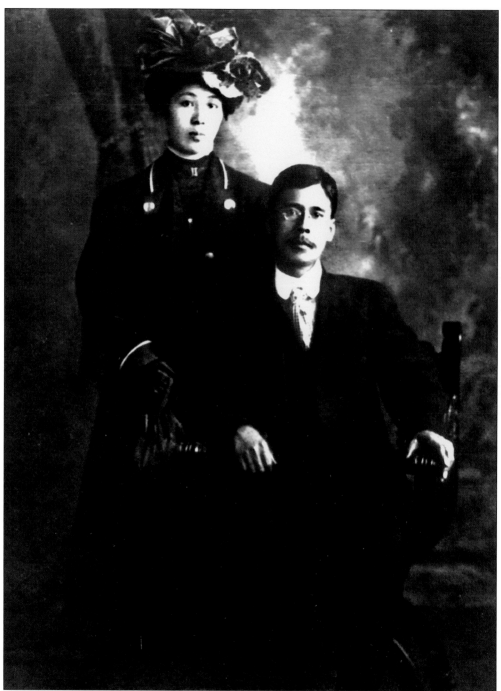

In December 1903, Joseph Sakai, a thoughtful and industrious young Japanese man with a degree from New York University School of Finance, presented himself to Rickards with his proposal for a colony of Japanese agricultural workers. Rickards and Sakai agreed on a piece of land, and by the next year, workers had arrived to begin cultivating the ground at the Yamato colony. Sakai sent for his wife Sada to join him, and other men sent for their wives, as well. The photo shows Sada and Joseph Sakai. (Photograph courtesy of Morikami Gardens and Museum.)

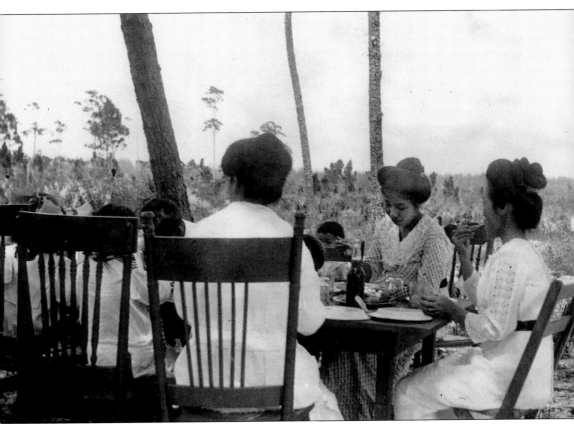

Life in the Yamato colony was hard and required many sacrifices, but the women of the colony did what they could to uphold the traditions and practices of their homeland. In this picture, they lunch al fresco with their children at a picnic table adjacent to the fields. Because of the hard work and skill of the workers, the colony prospered, growing pineapples, citrus, and a variety of vegetables. (Photograph courtesy of Morikami Gardens and Museum.)

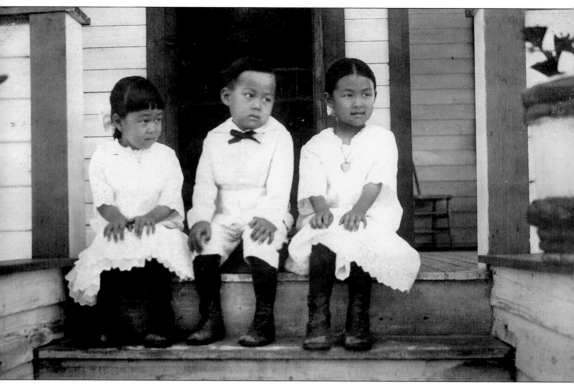

As the Yamato colony prospered, it grew in other ways, too. From left to right, Mishi, Rokuo, and Masa Kamiya were among the children who grew up in the colony. The colony's fortunes took a turn for the worse in late 1908, when a blight decimated the pineapple crop. Nationally, anti-Japanese feelings had begun to foment, making times more harsh and isolated for the men, women, and children of Yamato colony. Joseph Sakai died in 1923 and many of the colonists returned home.

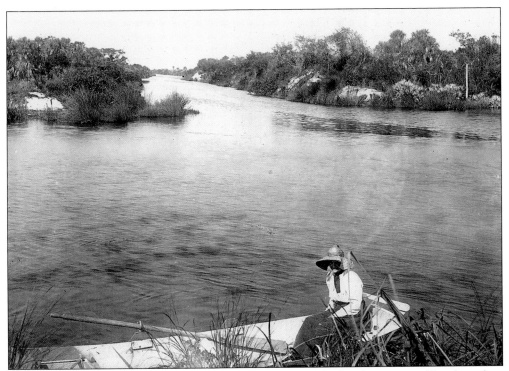

In the winter of 1898–1899 brawny, rawboned Frank Howard Chesebro came to Florida, sailing from the Volusia County area to Key West and back. He stopped along the way to visit the young community of Boca Raton and liked what he saw. Four years later, he returned and found things even more to his liking. He bought 60 acres of scrub pine–covered land and then more after he returned with his family. He and his wife, Jeanette—better known as "Nettie"—had three children: son Harry and daughters Ruth and Esther. In the picture, Nettie Chesebro waits for her oarsman at the Hillsboro River at the Florida East Coast Canal.

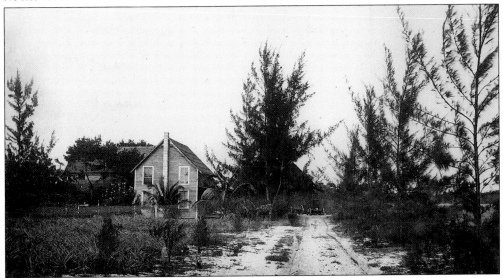

The Chesebro family's home was located between Dixie Highway and Federal Highway south of Camino Real.

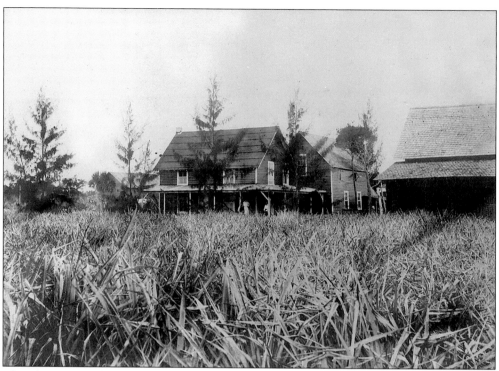

The Chesebro property was located where the Boca Raton Resort and Club and the Royal Palm Yacht and Country Club are now.

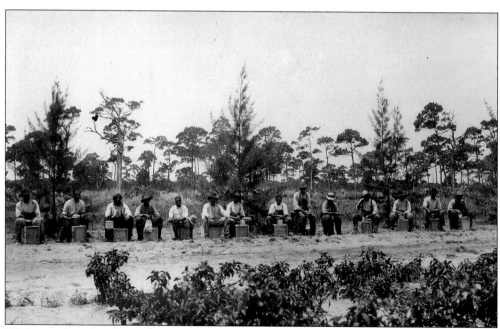

Workers at the Chesebro farm pause for lunch and a brief respite. The family farm employed many workers and grew potatoes, parsnips, tomatoes, onions, bananas, peas, beans, beets, and lettuce.

With the influx of
families into the
community, the
need for a school
arose. George Long,
Frank Chesebro,
and Bert Raulerson
led the effort to
bring a school to the
community, because
the daily ride to
Deerfield Beach
was a hardship.
Until a schoolhouse
could be erected,
Long offered a
room in his packing
house. The county
promised a teacher
if the community
provided the school.
Chesebro started the
actual work, clearing
the land. Building
materials were
donated by members
of the community.
Together they built
a one-room frame
building, which
Chesebro painted
white. In the picture,
children walk a path
through the scrub
oak to the school.

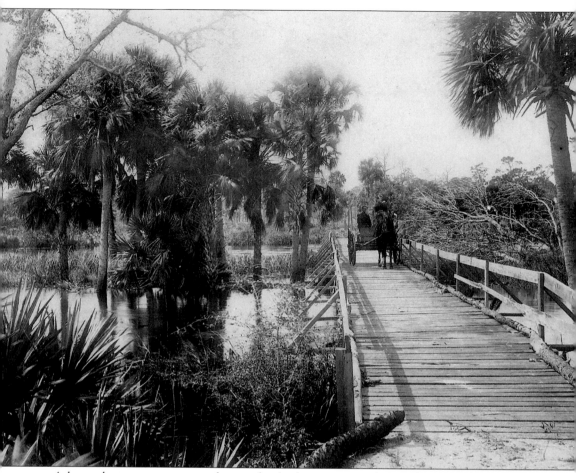

A horse-drawn wagon crosses the wooden bridge, spanning the north prong of the Hillsboro River, now called the El Rio Canal.

Two

GROWING PAINS
1910–1919

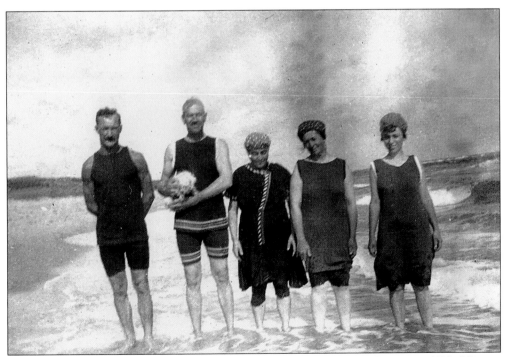

From left to right, Charles Schneider, George Race, Nellie Rose, Lizzie Brown, and Ethyl Brown enjoy a November day in the Boca Raton surf in 1917.

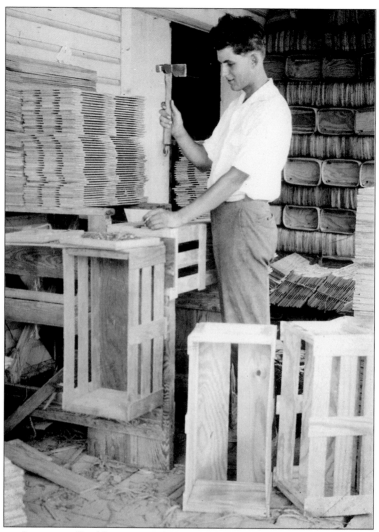

The two years Laurence Gould spent teaching at Boca Raton's one-room schoolhouse proved to be a springboard for an enlightened career. Gould, 18, had left his family's home in Lacota, Michigan, to teach for a few years so he could make enough money to study at the University of Michigan. The Chesebros invited him to Boca Raton to teach, succeeding Esther Chesebro as the school's teacher. Gould was its fifth teacher in its six years. He taught grades one through eight for two years. He and his students founded a newspaper, *The Boca Raton Semi-Occasional Newspaper.* Gould also taught Sunday school, organized community events, and fully reveled in his life in rural southern Florida. He went on to the University of Michigan and earned a doctorate in geology. He became a professor at Michigan, the University of Arizona, and Carleton College in Northfield, Minnesota, where he served as the college's president from 1945 to 1962. He also was involved in polar explorations, and Rear Adm. Richard E. Byrd tapped Gould to be his second in command for his first Antarctic exploration in 1928–1929. For his achievements, Gould received the Congressional Gold Medal and more than 30 honorary doctoral degrees. After his long career as a geologist, explorer, and educator, Laurence McKinley Gould died in 1999 at 98 years of age. In this picture, Gould assembles crates at Long's packing house. He taught in Boca Raton from 1914 to 1916 and many years later wrote to Boca Raton's archivist, "Indeed it seems to me that the only memories I have of Boca Raton are pleasant."

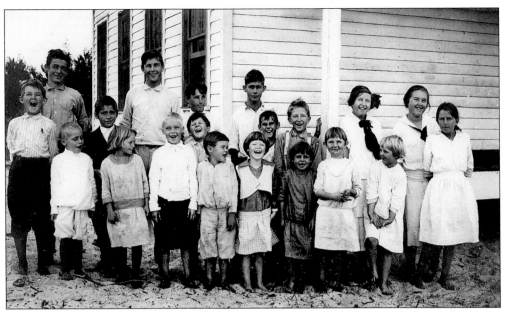

Gould poses with his students during his first year teaching in Boca Raton. He boarded with the Chesebros and rode with Charlie Raulerson in his covered wagon to pick up the children from their homes.

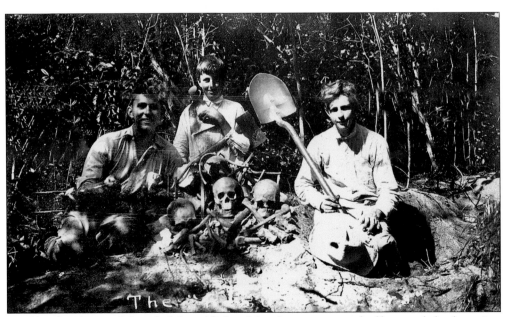

Gould, right, along with Joseph, left, and Robert Myrick, center, unearthed human skeletal remains. Gould insisted on sending some of the remains to the Smithsonian for analysis that revealed the remains were Indians who lived on the land before the arrival of European explorers.

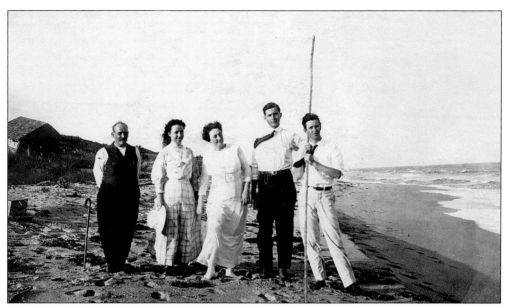

The fun-loving Myrick family didn't live in Boca Raton long, but they left an indelible mark. William L. Myrick and his wife Mamie moved to Boca Raton from Charlotte, North Carolina, in 1911. They had three children: Aldah, Joseph, and Robert. The beach held a special appeal to the Myricks. In this picture, Mamie Myrick, center, strolls the shore with friends.

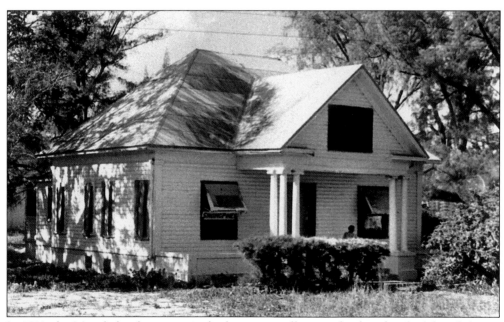

In 1914, the Myrick family constructed a home partially using lumber they had found during their many walks along the beach. The family pulled up stakes and moved to Dunedin in 1917 and sold the home at S.W. First Avenue and Third Street to George and Nelly Race and their daughter Lillian. The girl loved the sounds made by wind from the nearby pine trees as it whistled through the house, and she named the house Singing Pines.

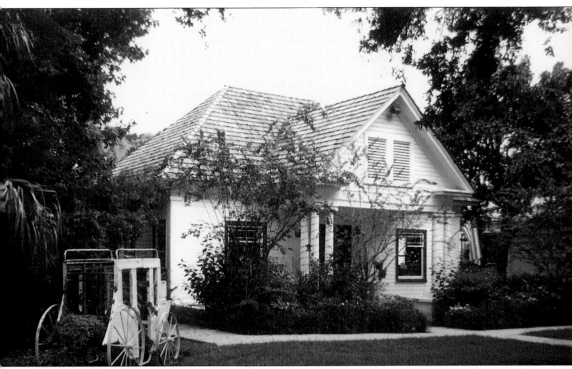

When Lillian Race Williams became too ill to live in the childhood home she loved, she moved to a convalescent home and Singing Pines was moved and renovated to become the home for the Boca Raton Children's Museum. The hands-on museum was opened to the public in 1979. The picture shows it as it appears today.

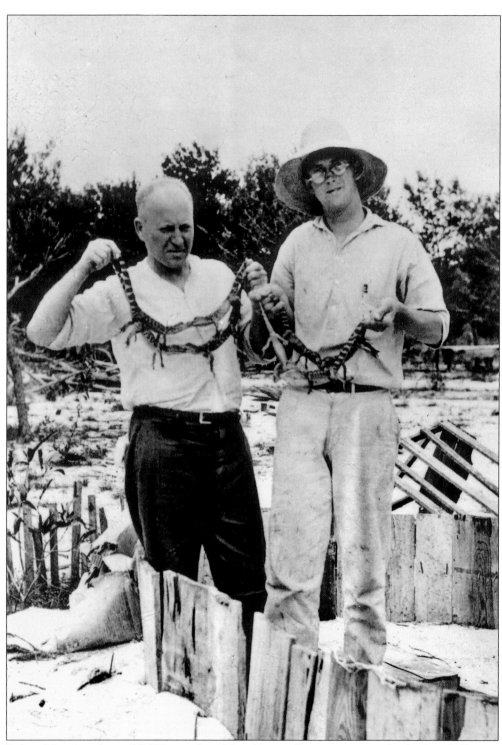

Robert Myrick, right, and Bill Young show Myrick's pet alligators, grown in his backyard alligator farm. Bill Young and his wife Margaret were Scots who moved to Florida so that Bill, a sculptor, could work on Vizcaya, the elaborate villa of industrialist James Deering.

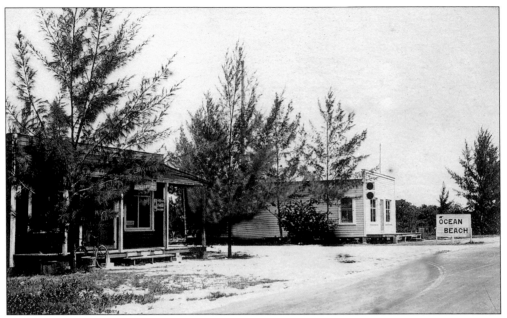

Bill Young and his wife Margaret, known to most as "Peg," moved to Boca Raton, where Peg opened a grocery store in 1915. She later also took on the job of postmistress after George Long relinquished the job after nine years. The post office is to the left in the picture and the store is to the right.

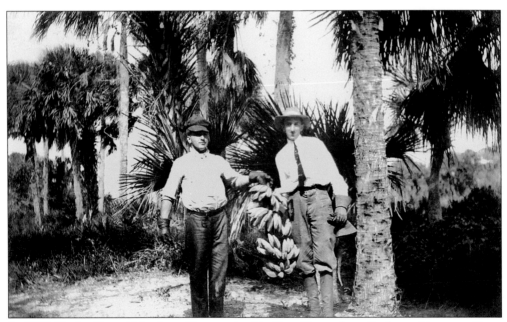

In 1913, Harley D. and Harriette Gates arrived in Boca Raton from Poultney, Vermont. Gates suffered from asthma and was urged to try Florida's warmer climate. Harley Gates is on the right, proudly displaying bananas grown on his property.

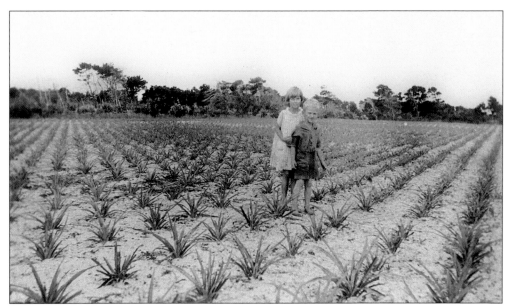

Harley and Henriette Gates's two children, Imogene Alice and Harley Parkhurst (Parkhurst was Henriette's maiden name), better known as Buddy, pose at the Chesebro pineapple plantation.

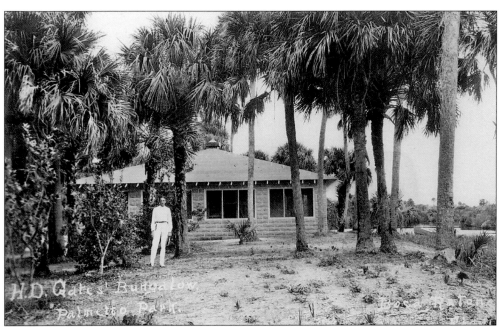

Gates, who served as the city's first judge, built a concrete home called Palmetto Park Plantation, located on the northwest bank of what is now Palmetto Park Road at the Intracoastal Waterway.

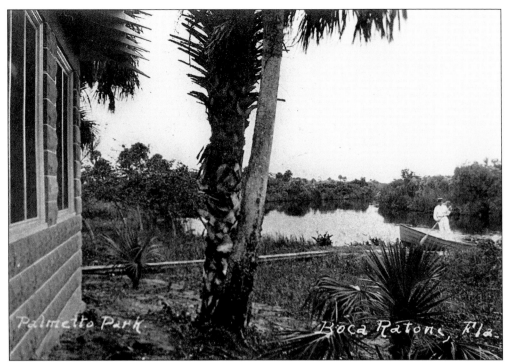

The view from Harley Gates's home was spectacular. He grew ornamental plants and fruit trees around the house.

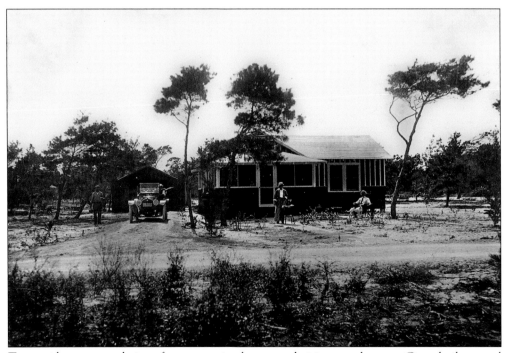

To provide accommodations for prospective buyers and visitors to the area, Gates built several guest bungalows and named them after U.S. states. This one is New York.

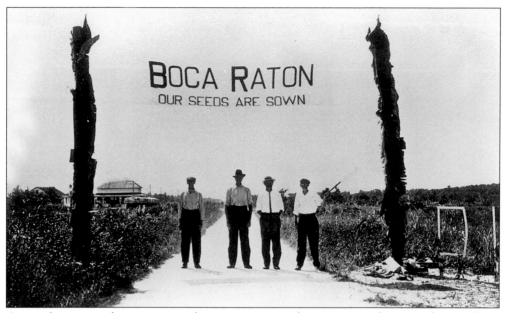

As people continued to migrate to the area, commerce began to grow, but agriculture in Boca Raton long remained a strong part of the community.

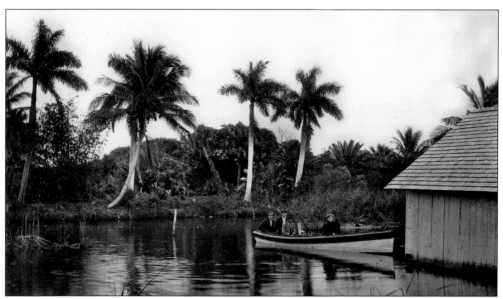

Even with a bit of nippy weather, the scenery was pleasing and the weather was nice enough for a bit of cruising near the former site of Thomas Rickards's canal house, which had been demolished by 1906. The boathouse at the right was located at the east end of what is now Royal Palm Road.

A young man looks over a huge pair of catfish caught in local waters. In fresh and saltwater, fishing remains a popular pastime in Boca Raton and all of Palm Beach County.

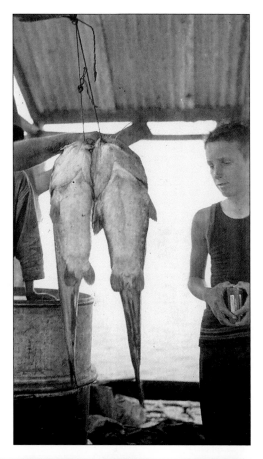

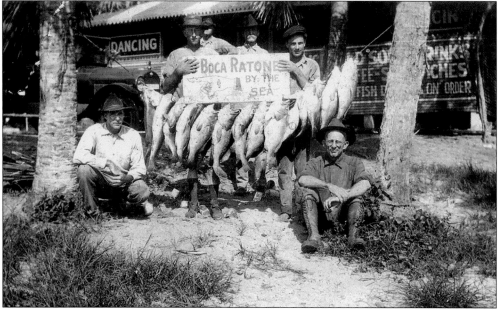

These anglers pose with their bountiful catch at the north side of the inlet about 1919.

COLORED AUCTION

PEARL CITY
NEXT MONDAY
April 26, 1 p. m.

FREE BOAT RIDE
No Children Taken on the Boat
Free Boat Leaves:
West Palm Beach, City Dock 8:00 a. m.
Boynton - - - 9:30 a. m.
Delray - - - 10:30 a. m.
BIG FREE FISH DINNER AT THE SALE

PEARL CITY A brand new town on the county road. For colored people--- one half mile north Boca Ratone. Beautiful site. Business lots and residence lots.

$5:00 Down, $5:00 Per Month
No Monthly Interest, No Taxes

GEO. A. LONG, Owner
Boca Ratone, Fla.

GEORGE FRYHOFER, Land Auctioneer
First National Bank Bldg., Chicago

Those Who Buy when a Town is First Opened up make the Money

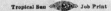
Tropical Sun Job Print

In 1914, George Long suggested to Thomas Rickards that the time was right to begin selling property to African Americans. Before that time, many of the blacks who worked in the fields lived in Deerfield Beach, others in Delray Beach. All had to endure a long wagon ride to work and home each day. A portion of Rickards's property was divided into lots and sold at auction. The resulting community was called Pearl City. Some say it was so named for Pearl Street, which ran through the community; others contend it was named for The Hawaiian Pearl pineapple, which was introduced to South Florida.

One of Pearl City's first land owners, and the first black man to reside in Boca Raton, was Alex Hughes, who worked at Chesebro's farm and went on to become a community activist and leader. Hughes Park, on the north side of Glades Road at Federal Highway, was dedicated in his honor in 1972.

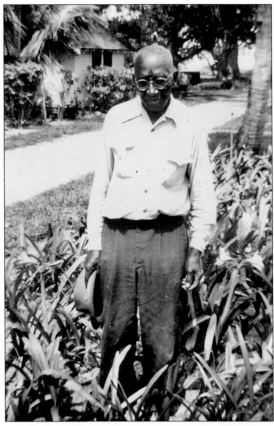

Work began on the first church in Pearl City, the Macedonia African Methodist Episcopal Church, in 1918.

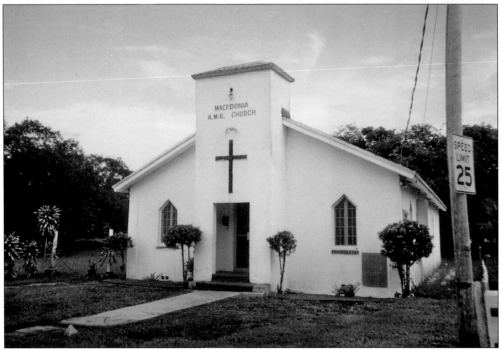

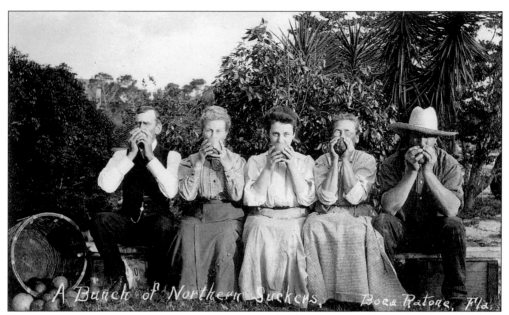

The opportunity to venture into a citrus grove and pick one's own fruit proved irresistible to many Northerners.

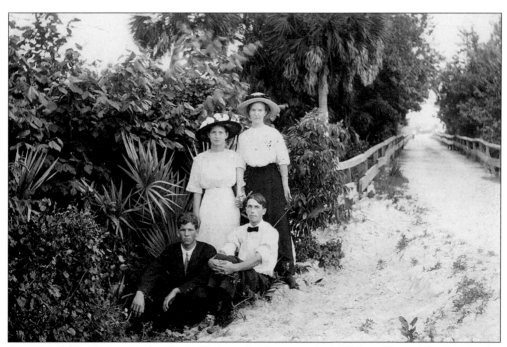

A group of friends pose at the Dixie Highway bridge over the Hillsboro River. The first bridge had been built in 1905. The second one was constructed in 1912.

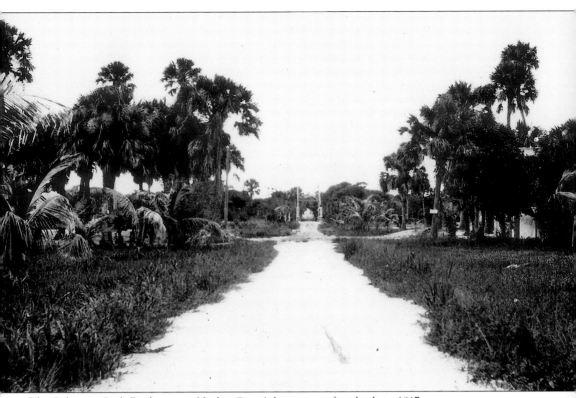

The Palmetto Park Bridge, near Harley Gates's home, was first built in 1917.

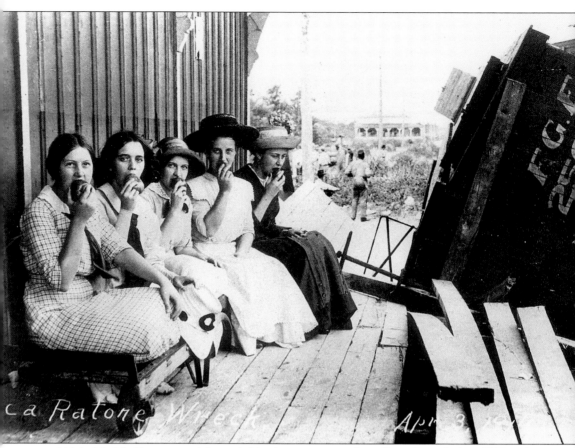

Aldah Myrick Overstreet, left, and friends enjoy a snack at Boca Raton's first FEC railway station, near an overturned freight car. George Long's packing house is visible in the distance.

Three

FROM BOOM TO BUST
1920–1929

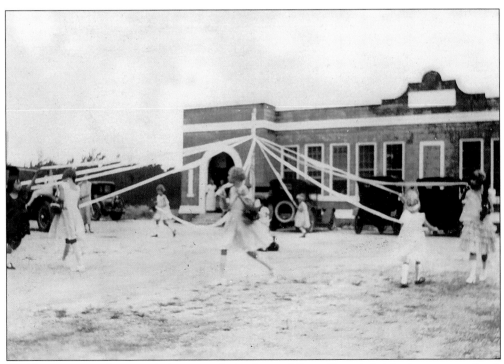

Children promenade around the maypole in front of Boca Raton's brick elementary school, which opened in 1920.

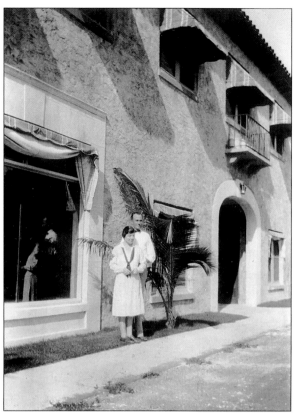

Jones Cleveland Mitchell, better known as J.C. or Joe, and his wife Floy Cooke Mitchell, arrived from Alabama in 1923 to develop 500 acres of land bought by Floy's father, LaFayette Cooke, where the Royal Palm Yacht and Country Club is now located. When LaFayette Cooke's health faltered, he sold his property, giving J.C. Mitchell the chance to go into real estate on his own. They built the Mitchell Arcade, which was formerly located at the southeast corner of the intersection of Dixie Highway and Palmetto Park Road, a prime location. The arcade had apartments upstairs and offices on the first floor. This picture of the Mitchells was taken at the arcade's southern façade.

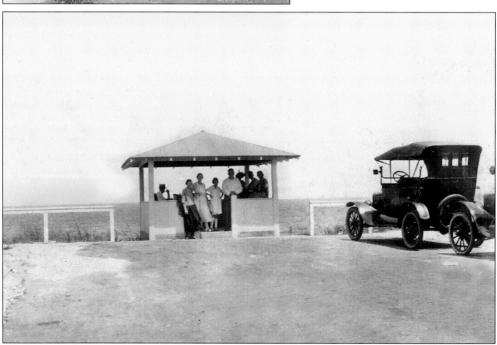

Going to the beach became more popular with the completion of a pavilion at Palmetto Park Road at the shore.

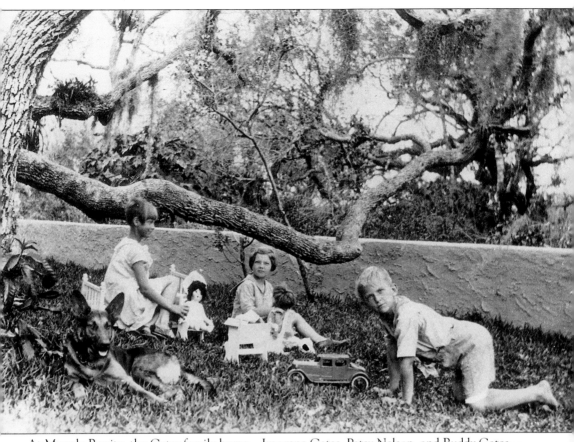

At Morada Bonita, the Gates family home—Imogene Gates, Patsy Nelson, and Buddy Gates—play under a gnarled oak tree.

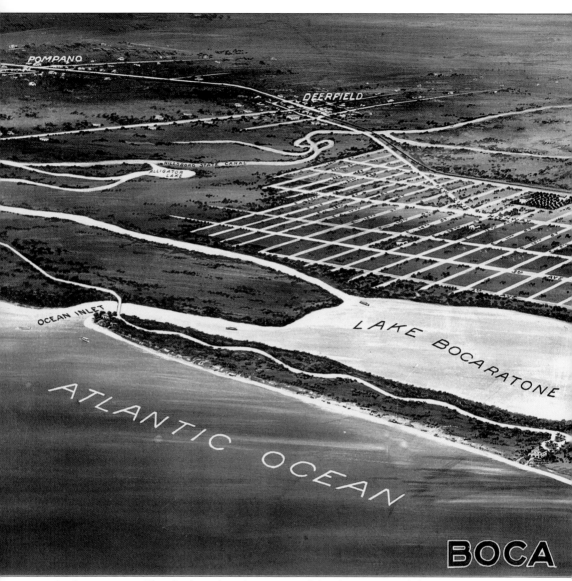

As the interest in Florida skyrocketed, a variety of developers created their visions for paradise-by-the-sea.

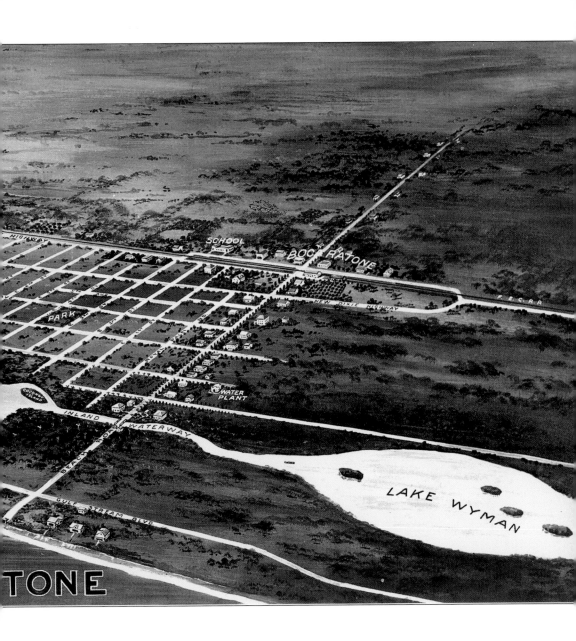

TONE

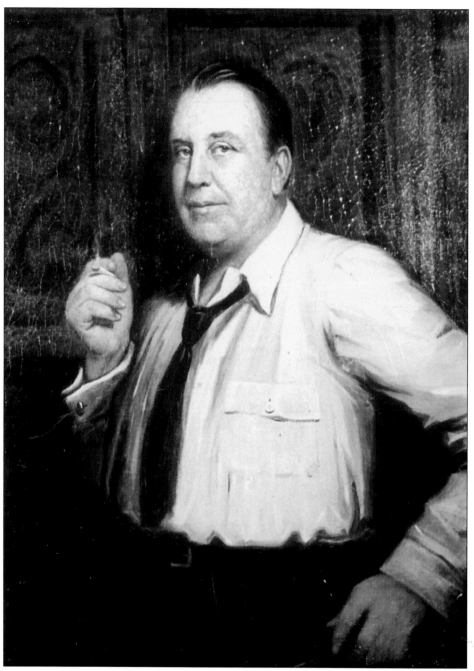

A native of Benicia, California, Addison Cairns Mizner was the seventh of eight children born to the Lansing Bond Mizner family of California pioneers. Addison Mizner went into architecture and became Florida's foremost designer of resort homes. His romantic mansion designs helped transform Palm Beach from an island of vacation cottages to the world's prime winter destination for the wealthy and famous. In 1925, at 53 and longing to design and create an entire city, he moved south to Boca Raton and set about developing 16,000 acres for residential and commercial use.

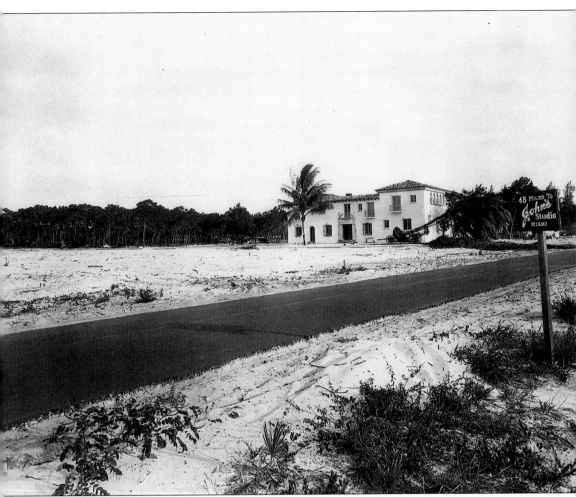

Mizner was determined to control all aspects of the manufacture of the buildings he designed. His Mizner Development Corporation had its headquarters at the corner of Dixie Highway and Camino Real. The two principal buildings were arranged to overlook a spacious courtyard. Construction of the northern building began in 1925 by Thomas L. Holland Construction Co. It housed the offices and showrooms where the public was welcomed. Construction on the southern building began several months after the first, in mid-summer 1925. The contractor was Harry Vought and Co. The south building housed the corporation's offices, drafting rooms, and engineering offices. At Mizner Industries in West Palm Beach, skilled craftsmen made furniture, roofing tiles, wrought-iron fixtures, urns, pottery, architectural embellishments, and hardware.

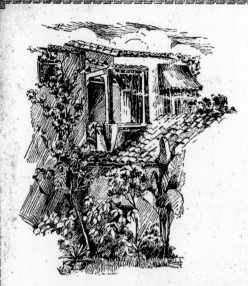

I Am the Greatest Resort in the World

I Am Boca Raton, Fla.

✑A FEW YEARS HENCE✑

✑I HAVE the combined charms of dignity, beauty and numerous attractions designed for fastidious people.

✕ ✕ ✕ ✕ ✕

I AM a place where people of taste can spend a few weeks, a season or the entire year in constant enjoyment.

✕ ✕ ✕ ✕ ✕

I OFFER the most even tempered climate in the world. I honestly believe I am the coolest place in the tropics.

✕ ✕ ✕ ✕ ✕

I CAN amuse people in many ways. I have as fine a bathing beach as can be found in the tropics. A magnificent Ritz-Carlton Hotel. A handsome Inn. Beautiful homes. Grand plazas, wide boulevards and streets. Colorful business sections. Theaters showing Broadway plays. Marvelous cabarets. Tennis courts everywhere, golf links, a polo field and a great landing field for airplanes.

✕ ✕ ✕ ✕ ✕

THIS is but a bare outline of what my future offers to the people who choose to live within my confines.

✕ ✕ ✕ ✕ ✕

MY future must be glorious. I have Addison Mizner to make it so.

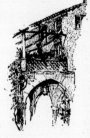

Mizner Development Corporation

PALM BEACH, FLORIDA   Developers of Boca Raton

Miami Temporary Offices, Ponce De Leon Hotel, Miami, Florida

MIAMI BEACH TEMPORARY OFFICE, 424 COLLINS AVENUE — TELEPHONE 888

Mizner used a barrage of advertising to promote his development, and his public relations consultant Harry Reichenbach's breathless prose conjured up vivid images to reel in prospective buyers. Boca Raton, boasted one of his brochures, was "Florida's wholly new entirely beautiful world resort."

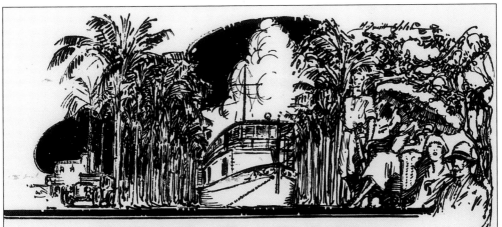

But for all their earnest appeal, Mizner's grandiose plans were built more on imagery than on substance. "My future must be glorious," the advertisement prompts, "I have Addison Mizner to make it so."

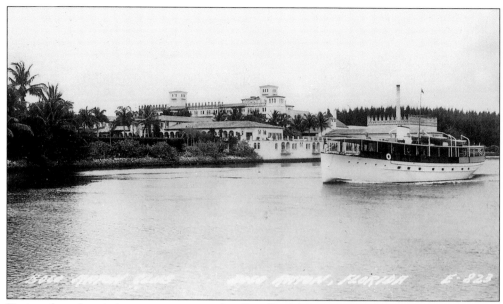

Designed as the city's centerpiece was the Castillo del Rey, or King's Castle, a 1,000-room oceanfront resort. The Ritz-Carlton hotel chain, seeing the area's potential, forged an agreement with Mizner to instead build a smaller but more luxurious resort that would take longer to complete. Anxious for a place to house his well-heeled guests, Mizner compromised with the Cloister Inn, built on the west side of Lake Boca Raton. It opened with 100 rooms on February 6, 1926. Now, after considerable expansion and several name changes, it operates as the Boca Raton Resort and Club.

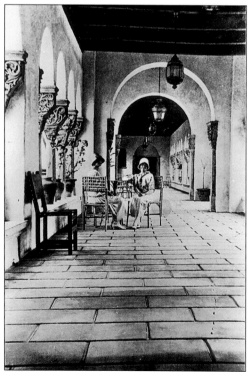

Mizner relied on many of the architectural fixtures he had used in Palm Beach to give the Cloister Inn its charm, blending Mediterranean Revival and Venetian styles. In this picture, Harriette Gates and Mary Driscoll chat at the inn's enclosed loggias.

This view of the fountain in the entrance plaza demonstrates some of the inn's Venetian influence in the window design and exterior furnishings.

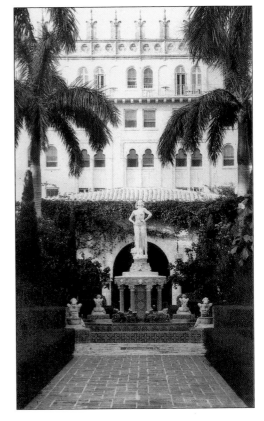

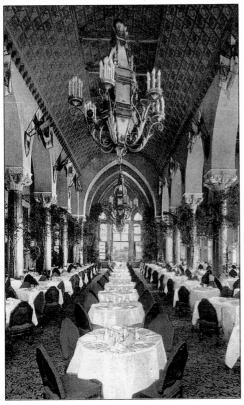

Mizner invited nearly 500 of South Florida's brightest social beacons to a grand-opening dinner and party. Among the guests were Edward and Eva Stotesbury, who had commissioned him to design their 37-room Palm Beach winter home, El Mirasol. Once open to the public, Cloister Inn guests could enjoy freshly caught seafood, prime meats, and fine wines in the beautifully appointed main dining room.

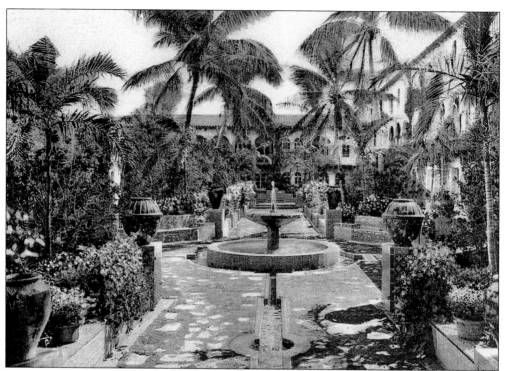

The Cloister Inn's patio was a delightful place for a stroll with fountains, palms, flowering plants, and places to sit and chat.

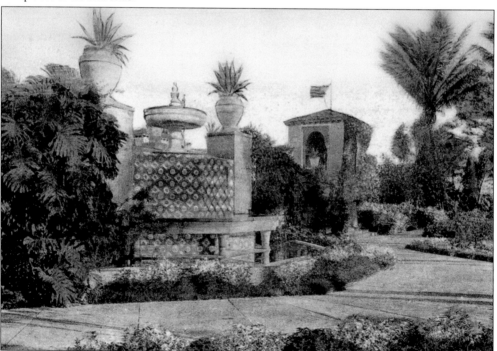

The area leading to the swimming pool featured hand-painted ceramic tiles, largely in blues and yellows.

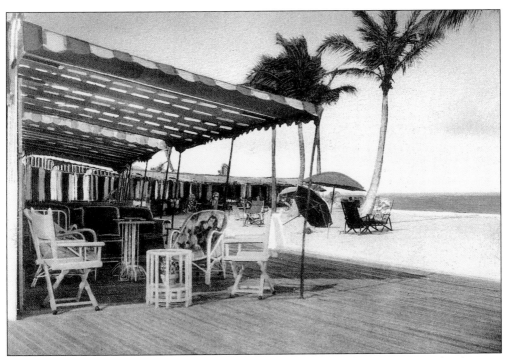

The cabanas allowed guests to enjoy the pleasures of the beach without giving up other luxuries offered by the inn.

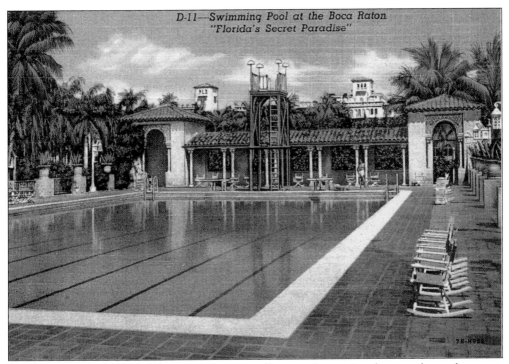

D-11—Swimming Pool at the Boca Raton
"Florida's Secret Paradise"

For guests who didn't want the inconvenience of hot sand, occasional seaweed, or salty water, the pool provided a refreshing alternative.

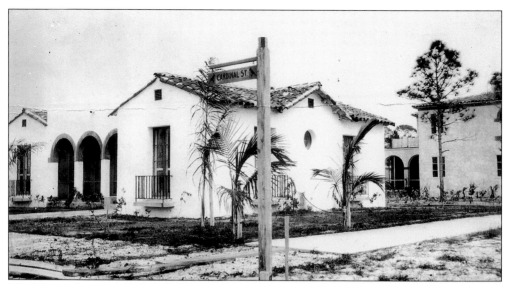

The Mizner plans included more than the resort. He also designed a pair of housing developments, Old Floresta and Spanish Village.

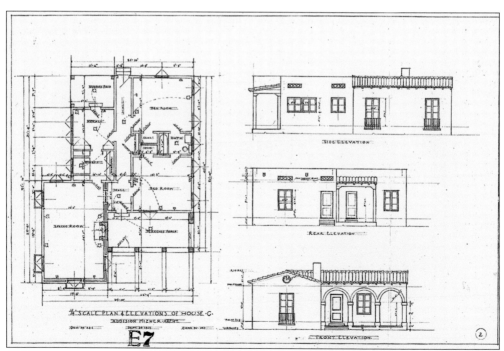

Old Floresta was an upscale subdivision with 10 model homes from which buyers could choose. This blueprint shows model G.

In July 1926, Mizner's grandiose dream turned into a nightmare with the collapse of 117 banks in Florida and Georgia. Mizner had borrowed heavily and squandered much of the money. Many of his brand-name backers pulled out and Mizner went bankrupt. Clarence H. Geist, one of the Mizner stockholders, did not bolt when times got tight. He liked Mizner's vision, but he had the acumen and restraint to get the job done right. In 1927, he acquired $7 million of the Mizner Development Corporation's debt and paid $71,000 for the Cloister Inn. The picture shows Geist and his wife Florence.

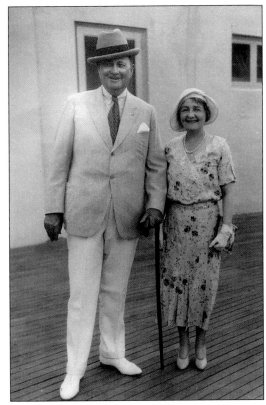

Among Mizner's projects that went unfinished as a result of his bankruptcy was Town Hall. Delray Beach architect William Alsmeyer stepped in to revise the plans, scale the project down, and see it to completion. In addition to the town's administrative offices, the building also housed the volunteer fire department and its 1926 LaFrance fire truck, "Old Betsy."

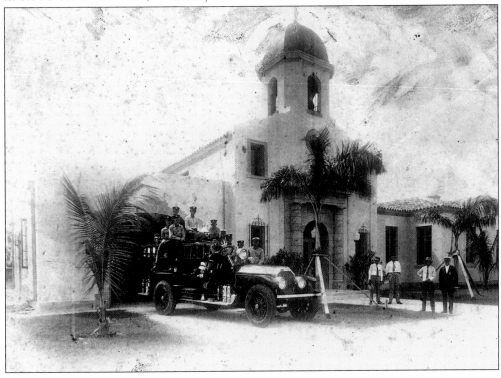

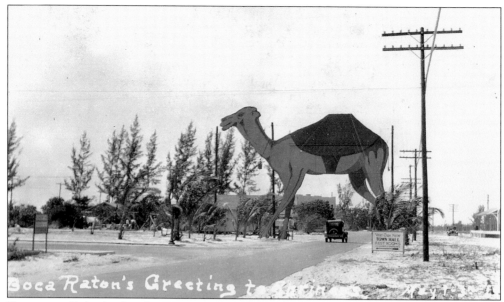

Trying to rally back after the community's setbacks due to Mizner's declaration of bankruptcy, chamber of commerce president J.C. Mitchell urged the town council to provide funds for construction of a giant camel. In the spring of 1928 the Shriners were holding their national convention in Miami and all participants who drove there had to take Dixie Highway. City fathers reasoned that since they had a virtually captive audience, a novelty such as the camel would heighten awareness of Boca Raton and perhaps spread word about the fledgling town.

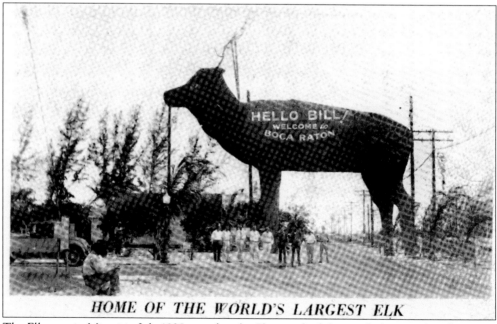

HOME OF THE WORLD'S LARGEST ELK

The Elks met in Miami in July 1928; so, after the Shriners had departed, the camel underwent a transformation, getting its hump flattened, a new paint job, and a set of ersatz antlers.

50

Four

BACK FROM ADVERSITY
1930–1939

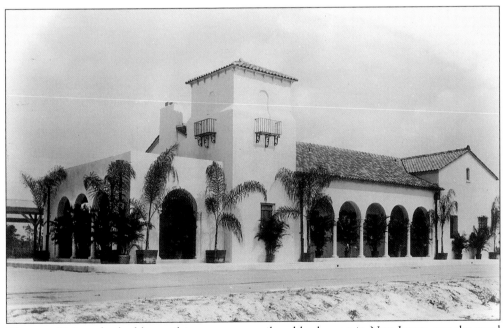

Clarence Geist, who had begun his career as a railroad brakeman in New Jersey, saw the need for a passenger depot to serve guests of the Boca Raton Club, which he expanded by adding 200 private beach cabanas and other amenities. Mizner had designed a passenger station but never got the chance to build it. Architect Chester G. Henninger tore a page from Mizner's sketchbook in creating the Mediterranean Revival–style depot, which was constructed in 1930.

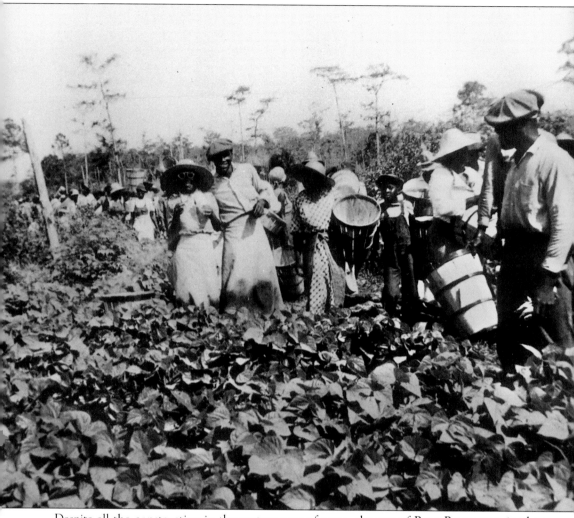

Despite all the construction in the eastern part of town, the rest of Boca Raton remained an active agricultural community. In 1933, August H. Butts of Fort Lauderdale took advantage of the economic downturn to purchase farmland cheaply, and his family's farm became one of the largest bean farms in the state. The farm used advanced growing methods and state-of-the-art watering systems to produce the best-tasting beans in the area. The farm hired local workers and migrants to meet their labor needs and had up to 400 workers in the fields during the height of the season. The area near where Town Center Mall stands was formerly part of the Butts farm.

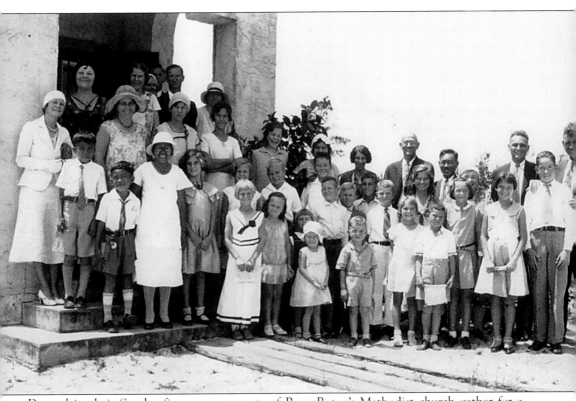

Dressed in their Sunday finery, congregants of Boca Raton's Methodist church gather for a group photo on a lovely spring day in April 1932.

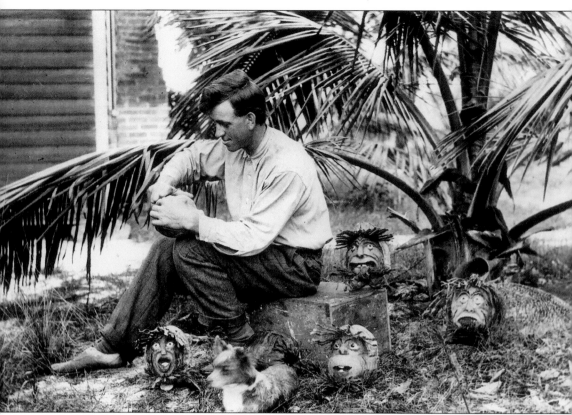

Harry Chesebro carved faces into coconuts and sold them at roadside fruit stands. After cutting out the features from the pithy outer layer of the coconut, Chesebro would add bits of broken shells for teeth and decorate by painting. The souvenirs—often found at roadside stands, along with fruit, nuts, candy, tiny orange crates filled with bubble gum, and other bric-a-brac—are still sold in Florida today.

Five

TIMES OF CHALLENGE 1940–1949

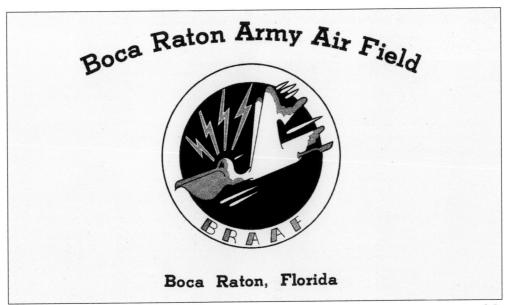

When the United States entered World War II in December 1941, Boca Raton's mayor, J.C. Mitchell, saw opportunity. Mitchell traveled to Washington to convince military officials that his seaside town had just what they needed. The new field of Radio Detection and Ranging— RADAR—was proving itself popular, and the military was trying to train new technicians as quickly as possible. For a variety of reasons, including the town's airport and the area's good weather, Boca Raton got the nod. The army acquired 5,860 acres for the base. The Boca Raton Club was turned into a housing facility for officers. Workmen painted the pastel walls gray and covered up the artwork and ornate furniture, putting them in storage until the hostilities ended. Trainees were housed in wooden barracks built on the base. More than 32,000 men and women received training at the air field.

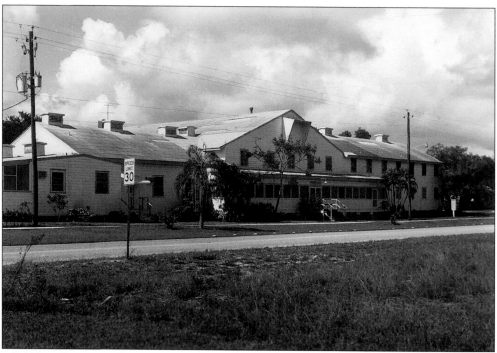

What later became known as Moody Hall originally served as a mess hall at the Boca Raton Army Air Field.

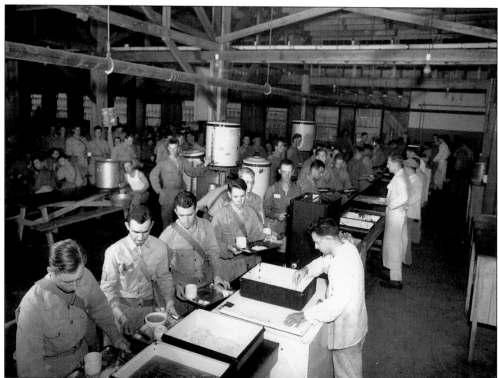

Soldiers line up for chow inside the base's mess hall.

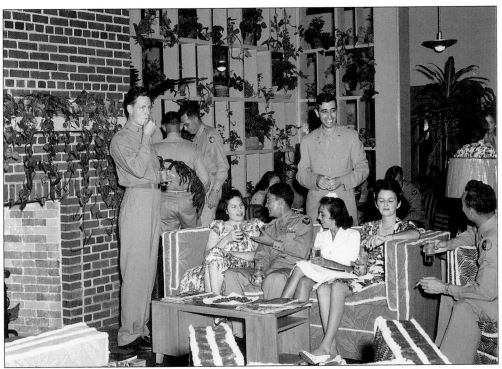

Officers and their guests enjoyed many of the comforts of home at the base's officers' club.

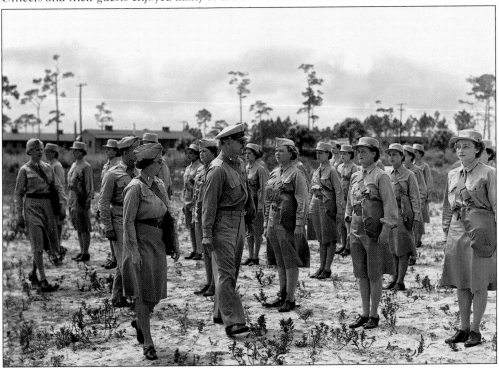

Women soldiers stand at attention during inspection. They served in several non-combat roles, primarily as nurses.

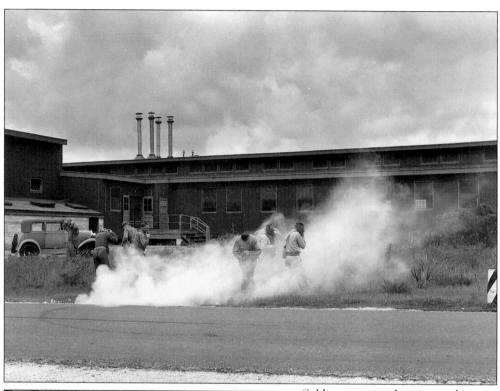

Soldiers practice donning and removing their masks in anticipation of exposure to toxic gases.

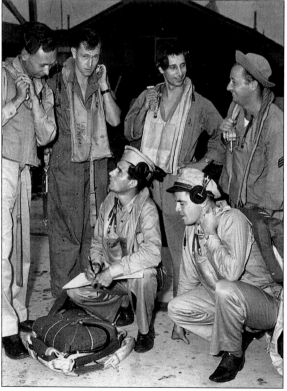

Lt. Manuel Chavez briefs his flight crew in preparation for undertaking an anti-submarine mission.

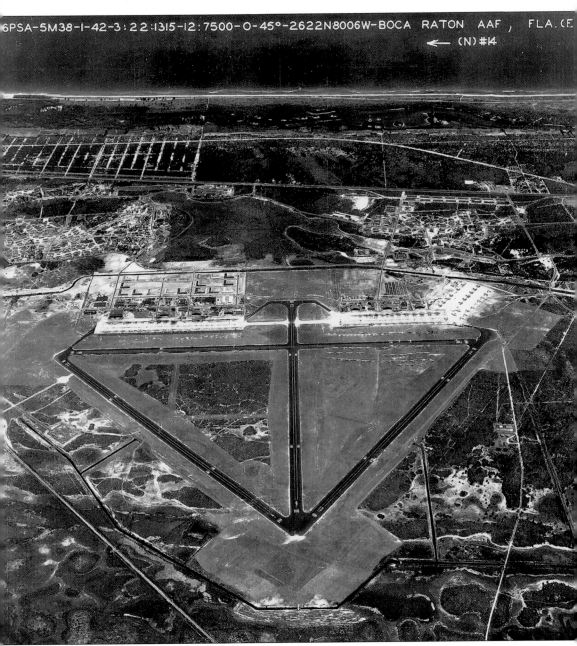

After the war's end, the city purchased property from the air base and agreed to construct a general aviation airport there.

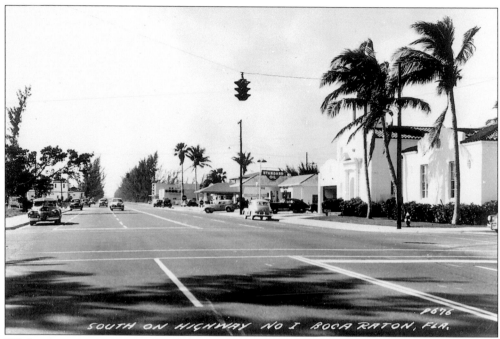

While many communities suffered during the war, Boca Raton fared well. There were more jobs available than civilian contractors could handle, and the businesses in the community enjoyed brisk business from the influx of the military. This picture is a view looking south on Federal Highway. The Town Hall is at the extreme right of the frame.

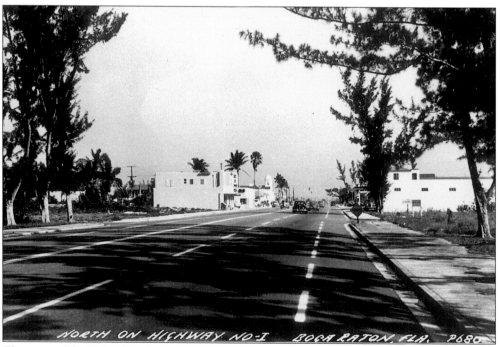

This view of the Federal Highway business district looks north. Town Hall's cupola is visible just to the left of the center.

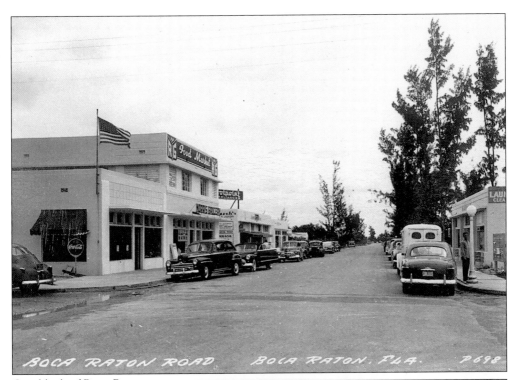

BOCA RATON ROAD   BOCA RATON, FLA.   P698

One block of Boca Raton Road was also part of the downtown business district, with the post office, Norris' grocery, and a laundry.

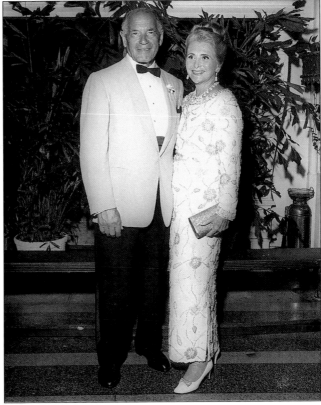

J. Myer Schine purchased the Boca Raton Club and other land holdings in Boca Raton from the estate of Clarence Geist. Schine reopened the club as the Boca Raton Hotel in 1945. With him in the picture is his wife Hildegarde, who remained active in Boca Raton's social and philanthropic circles long after her husband's death. (Photograph by Jim Leo.)

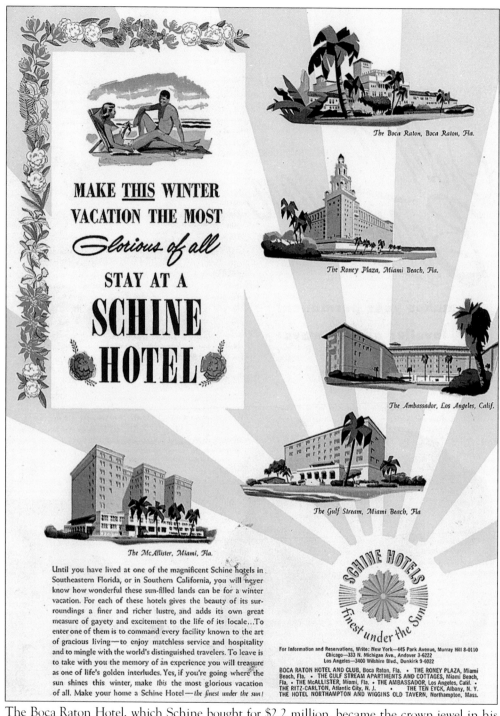

The Boca Raton Hotel, which Schine bought for $2.2 million, became the crown jewel in his chain of hotels. J. Myer Schine died in 1971. Hildegarde Schine lived to 1994. She was 91 at the time of her death.

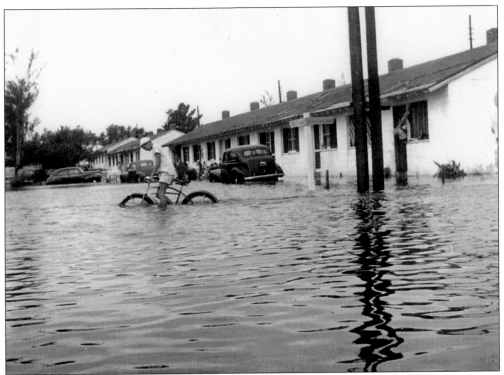

The third and fourth hurricanes of the 1947 season went aground at Boca Raton within 10 days of each other. The first storm carried maximum winds of about 100 miles per hour. The second one was significantly stronger. Water damage was widespread, as the scene at the Garden Apartments demonstrates.

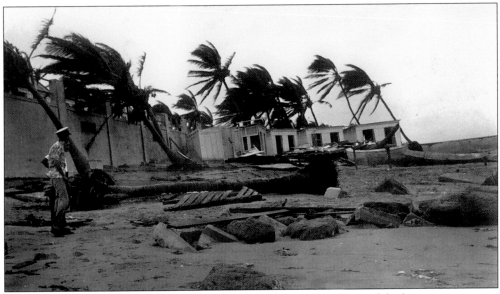

Wind damage was significant, too. The cabana club shows the effects of the battering.

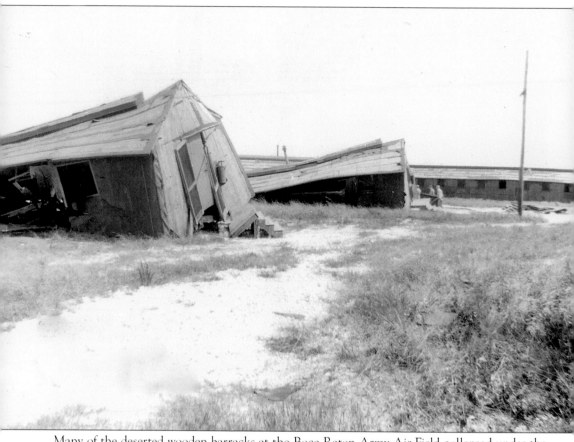

Many of the deserted wooden barracks at the Boca Raton Army Air Field collapsed under the force of the winds.

Six

GROWTH
AND GRANDEUR
1950–1959

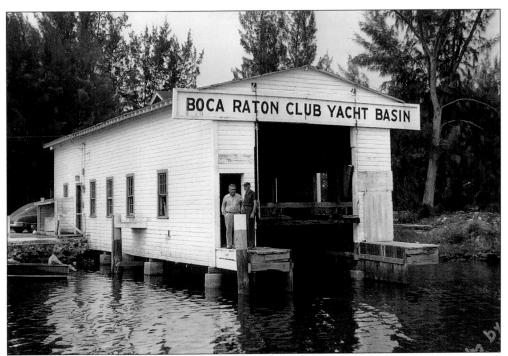

The sign at a boathouse south of the Camino Real Bridge was sure to provoke a few chuckles.
(Photograph by Jim Leo.)

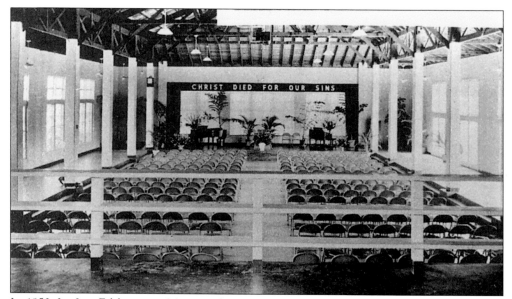

In 1950, Ira Lee Eshleman, a Miami radio minister, went looking for a place to build a Bible conference center. An acquaintance told him of the radar base in Boca Raton and he paid a visit. The place was a mess, with collapsed barracks from the 1947 hurricanes left rotting in the sun. Still, Eshleman liked the property and saw its potential. It had good roads, sewers, water mains, and electricity. He met with Mayor J.C. Mitchell outside the Mitchell Arcade and quickly hammered out the arrangements. Eshleman would pay $50,000 for 30 acres and 2 buildings. Eshleman paid $1,000 down. That investment has paid off in the form of Bibletown, the non-denominational Boca Raton Community Church, and Boca Raton Christian School.

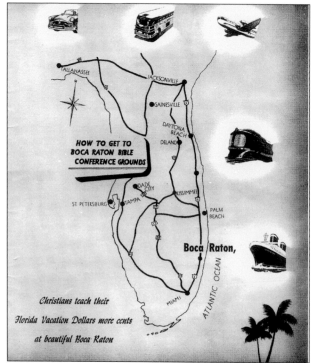

Its Florida location has made Bibletown popular with northerners, and its location midway between Miami and West Palm Beach makes it easy to reach for worshippers in southeast Florida.

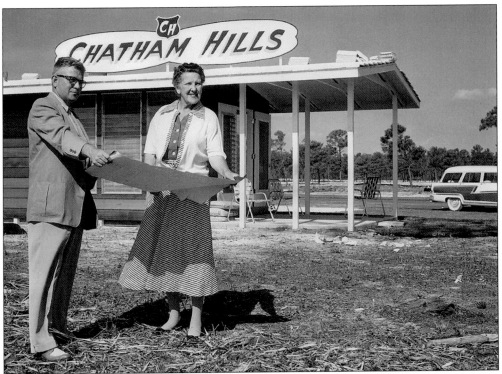

With the war over, the economy growing, and the baby boom underway, Florida's real estate market was back in bloom. In this picture, Lucius D. Schluesmeyer of Boca Raton Resort Properties, Inc., shows off the plans for Chatham Hills, an 80-acre development in northern Boca Raton.

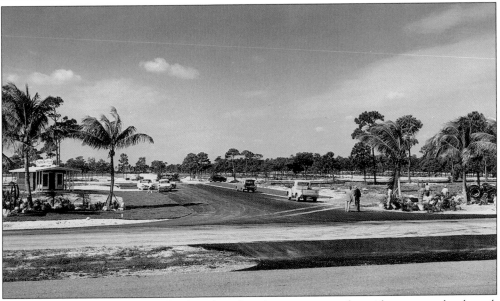

Chatham Hills featured high, dry lots dotted with pine trees and a wide entrance boulevard. The development was located between Federal and Dixie Highways between Twenty-eighth and Thirty-second Streets.

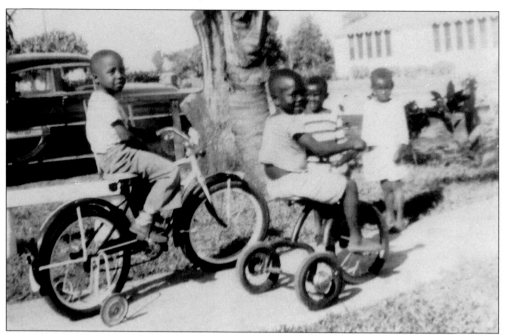

Gary Dolphus, left, on bicycle, and Leroy Miller, on tricycle, head for classes at the Boca Raton Negro School. The school was later known as Roadman School, named for Boca Raton council member Frank C. Roadman. The school, located at 1250 North Dixie Highway at the intersection with Ruby Street, was built in the late 1930s and remained open until 1964.

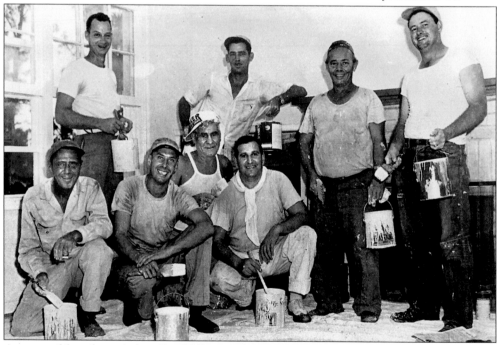

A group of friends, including Ray Hillegas, Johnny LaMont, Earl Troxell, Len Harris, Johnny Olsson, and Ray Roseke, pitch in to help Bill Eubank (rear left), whose home had been damaged by fire.

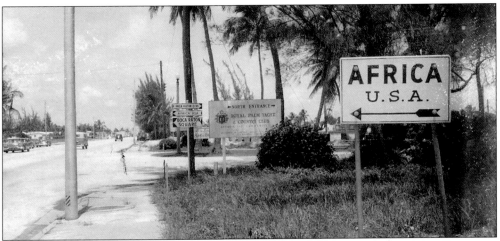

Late in the 1940s, entrepreneur John P. Pedersen fell in love with the area's natural beauty but found it a bit too quiet for his tastes. He told a local shopkeeper "This is the deadest town I've ever seen." John Pedersen and his wife Lillian turned their cottage industry—Lillian made decorative curtain tie-backs—into a profitable manufacturing company. The capital the Pedersens raised allowed them to go into real estate and development. After suffering a back injury at a worksite, John Pedersen was urged to give Florida's warm climate a try. A drive through lush, verdant Boca Raton reminded him of his studies of Africa and sparked an idea. In mid-January 1951, he purchased 350 acres of land at a city auction, paying about $25 an acre. He enlisted the help of son Jack, an architect, transforming the palmetto-covered acreage to a South Florida veldt. Africa-U.S.A. was a premier Florida attraction from February 1953 to September 1961. The park averaged more than 2,000 visitors daily, who rode the trams, strolled through the diamond exhibit, and watched the Watusi geyser in the middle of Lake Nanyki spew water 160 feet into the air every hour.

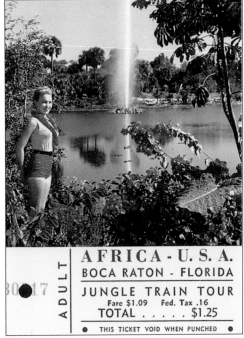

Pedersen issued postcard tickets to Africa-U.S.A. Once the card was punched, it was no longer valid for entry to the park but made a dandy souvenir. This card shows the Watusi geyser, which erupted every hour, spewing a thousand gallons of water per minute 160 feet into the air.

AFRICA - U.S.A.
BOCA RATON - FLORIDA
ADULT
30●17
JUNGLE TRAIN TOUR
Fare $1.09   Fed. Tax .16
TOTAL $1.25
● THIS TICKET VOID WHEN PUNCHED ●

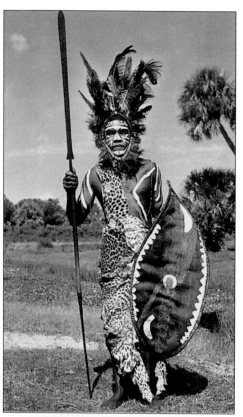

Machakas, a tall Masai warrior clad in a leopard skin carrying a rhino-hide shield, met guests at the entrance to the Tanganyika Territory section of Africa-U.S.A., billed as "Florida's fabulous uncaged zoo."

A Jeep safari and mini-trains each holding 50 guests took visitors through Africa-U.S.A.'s 350 acres, including a stop at Jungletown, a replica of an African village with authentic mud-and-thatch huts.

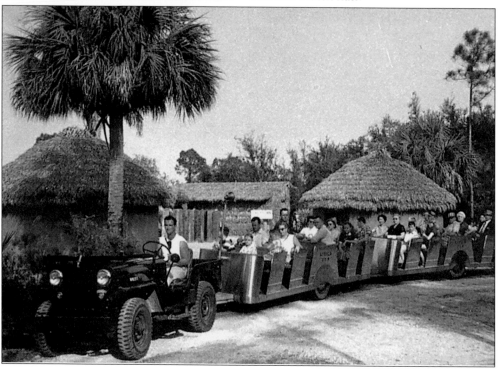

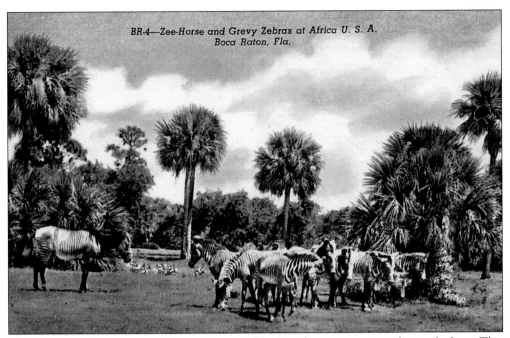

BR-4—Zee-Horse and Grevy Zebras at Africa U. S. A.
Boca Raton, Fla.

The tours gave visitors an up-close-and-personal look at the many species of animals there. This card shows a zee-horse and banjo-eared Grevy zebras. Other less-common species included the aoudads and king-sized antelopes called elands.

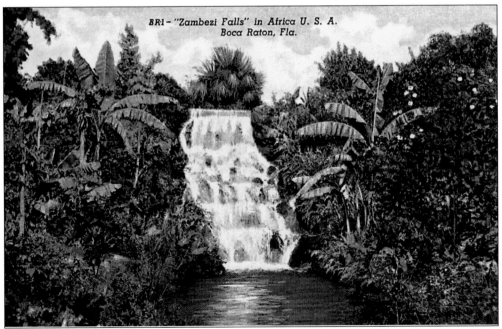

BR-1 – "Zambezi Falls" in Africa U. S. A.
Boca Raton, Fla.

Originally intended as a botanical garden, Africa-U.S.A. was filled with 55,000 exotic and flowering plants. Many of the plants came from a Wilton Manors nursery, owned and operated by John Pedersen's daughter and son-in-law, Shirley and George Schneider. The area around Zambezi Falls, a 35-foot waterfall, showed off the fabulous flora.

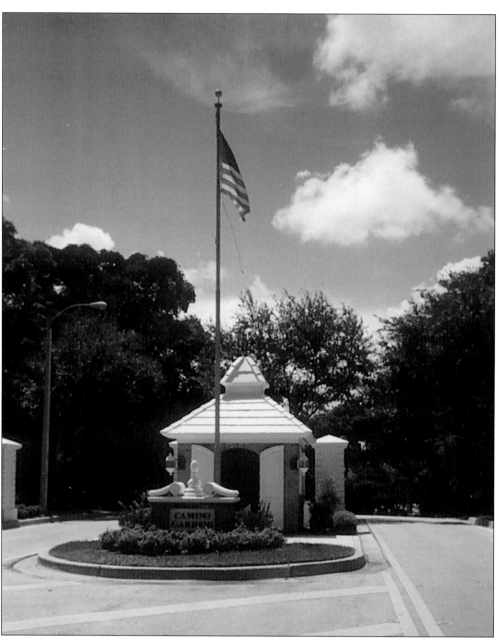

Throughout Africa-U.S.A.'s existence, Pedersen was hounded by the Federal Department of Agriculture. After Pederson prevailed in a two-year battle over the importation of giraffes, inspectors found an infestation of African red ticks on the animals. Spraying for the ticks killed many animals and Pedersen could stand no more. He turned the operation over to a corporation, but after two years he took it back and closed the attraction. Animals were sold to zoos, other attractions, and private collectors, and the gates of Africa-U.S.A. shut permanently on September 4, 1961. The Camino Gardens subdivision was built where Africa-U.S.A. had stood. In 2003, the Camino Gardens Association erected a permanent plaque commemorating the 50th anniversary of the opening of Africa-U.S.A. The picture shows the Camino Gardens gatehouse.

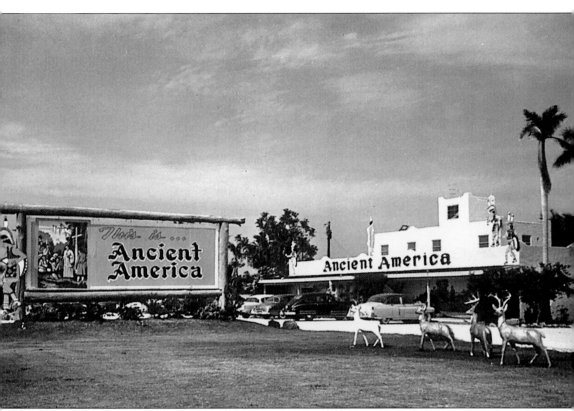

In northern Boca Raton, Esmond G. Barnhill, a peripatetic photographer and photo tinter from St. Petersburg, bought 24 acres where Indian burial mounds were found. Archeologists thoroughly investigated the mounds, and after they had completed their work, Barnhill created an attraction that preserved the mounds and taught visitors about the life and lore of the area. He called it Ancient America.

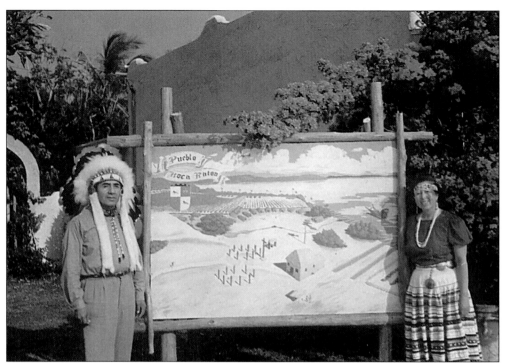

Ancient America boasted of a wide collection of artifacts including doubloons, pirate chests, shrunken heads, arrowheads, and chain-mail armor.

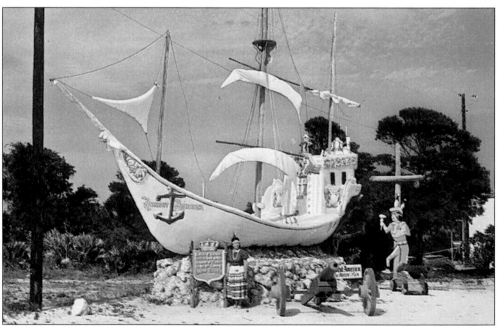

A stone replica of a Spanish galleon used in the 15th-century conquest was supposed to help attract customers. Disillusioned at the dearth of history-loving visitors, Barnhill shut down Ancient America in 1958. The Sanctuary, an exclusive gated community, was built on the site, but the mounds still remain.

BOCA RATON NEWS

Serving Boca Raton and Deerfield Beach

VOL. 1 NO. 1   Boca Raton, Florida, Friday, December 2, 1955   PRICE 10¢

Town Council Approves Sale Of $325,000 Revenue Bonds

The Boca Raton Town Council in an adjourned meeting, Tuesday night, accepted a joint bid of Mullaney Wells and Co. and Sullivan, Nelson and Goss for the purchase of the new $325,000 water and sewer revenue certificate issue. The funds will be used to defray costs of improving, extending and maintaining the municipally-owned system.

The bid called for an annual interest rate of 3.570% per cent. Bonds will mature annually between 1959 and 1985.

A total of five bids were opened and considered.

A second set of sealed bids for water system construction was opened and referred to the town's consulting engineer for study.

Other action included: Authorization of payment of $200 to the Seacrest Band Boosters Club; payment of rent to the Lions Club for use of the building for the teen-agers; payment of $13,347 to the consulting engineer for work on the water and sewer expansion program.

The council said it will meet with the Planning and Zoning Board to look over the new zoning ordinance and district map before the final public hearing.

The request for property in Section 30, west of the F.E.C. Railway, to be zoned business, commercial or industrial was referred to the planning board.

Christmas Lights Turned on Nov. 21

Mayor Harold Turner, Charles Senior of the Florida Power and Light Co., Fred Jungbluth, chairman of the Christmas lighting program and Otto Yark, president of the Chamber of Commerce, participated in the "turning on of lights" Nov. 21. The ceremony took place in Sanborn Square.

The lights were installed by Eubank Electric Co. The town council has voted to pay for the installation of the lights. The Chamber of Commerce store lighting contest is taking shape as more merchants are entering each week.

Christmas Arrangements For Garden Club Meet

The Boca Raton Garden Club will meet at the Lions Club, Dec. 6, at 2 p.m. Mrs. H.I. Gallup, horticulture chairman, has chosen "This Month in the Garden" as the theme for December.

The Christmas arrangements made at the workshop at Mrs. Conrad Sederlund's on Nov. 29 will be displayed. Mrs. W. Livington, arrangements chairman, and her committee will give a demonstration on "Beauty and Simplicity for the Holiday Season" using materials gathered from the fields.

Follow hometown activities Subscribe to the Boca Raton News

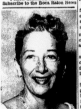

MRS. MacSPADDEN
— Art Guild President

William Herbold Elected Mayor At Council Organzational Meet

William Herbold was elected mayor of Boca Raton at the organizational meeting yesterday morning. L.A. Zimmerman was elected first vice mayor and Melvin Schmitt, second vice mayor. H.D. Gates was appointed municipal judge and the firm of Lilienthal and Johnston were retained as town attorneys.

Committee appointments were public safety, police and fire, Schmitt, Harold Turner and Herbold; public utilities, water, sewer, airport and sanitation, Zimmerman, Andrew Brennan and Herbold; public service, streets, parks, marine affairs, cemetery and maintenance of public buildings, Turner Schmitt and Herbold; administration, finance, engineering inspection, legal, engineering inspection, Brennan, Zimmerman and Herbold.

The council decided that the town's funds will remain with the First National Bank of Delray Beach and the Atlantic National Bank of West Palm Beach.

The retiring council held a brief meeting prior to the administering of oaths by Miss Ruth Lawson, notary public, to the new councilmen.

Retiring Mayor Harold Turner thanked the council for the co-operation shown during the past year.

MAYOR HERBOLD

Many To Get This Newspaper

More than 1,200 copies of this first issue of the Boca Raton News will go today to the residents of the Boca Raton and Deerfield Beach area, to the Florida university journalism schools, to the Florida Press Association, Northern advertising agencies and numerous others the publishers think will be interested in this newspaper.

Publishers of the new newspaper are Robert L. and Lora S. Britt and editor is Margaret Olsson, pioneer Boca Raton resident.

Papers of incorporation have been filed in Tallahassee. Officers are the publishers and Otto Yark of Boca Raton. Other stockholders are all local men and women.

The response to the establishing of a newspaper in Boca Raton can be seen in the large number of good wishes expressed throughout this issue by the business people of the community by paid advertisements.

Temporary office of the Boca Raton News is at the Olasor house, N. Federal Hwy. The mailing address is P.O. Box 1157.

Boys Practice for Midget Football Game; Queen Will Be Selected

Boys of the seventh and eighth grades are participating in the midget football game to be held at the Seacrest athletic field, Friday, Dec. 9, at 7:30 p.m.

John Hager, Boca Raton, is assisting Bob Bird of Delray Beach and Jack Clapp of Boynton in coaching the boys. Clapp was selected as head coach.

Uniforms were issued to the boys on Monday. Proceeds from this game will be used to provide football uniforms for a Midget Football League in the south county area.

The entire coaching staff of Seacrest High School is co-operating and the school is making available equipment and facilities. Seacrest is asking for none of the proceeds except the costs of cleaning equipment.

A Midget Football Game queen will be selected from one of the three schools. A girl in each of the seventh and eighth grades will be selected as queen candidate contestants. The girl who receives the highest number of votes out of the three schools will be queen. The girls in each of the two remaining schools who receives the highest number of votes will be chosen as the queen's attendants. Votes will be based on ticket sales.

Each ticket sold will count as one vote. Each student selling tickets will vote for the candidate of his or her choice by writing the name of the respective candidate for queen on the back of the ticket stub. All stubs that are to count for votes must be in the office by Thursday morning, Dec. 8.

Open House Dec. 4

December 4 is open house at the new Holy Cross Hospital, Oakland Park, 10 a.m. to 10 p.m. Everyone is invited to attend.

Library and Cultural Arts Center Will Serve Entire Community

The proposed Boca Raton Library and Cultural Art Center will bring to this section one of the most complete buildings of its kind in South Florida.

Books and art will receive first attention with plans included for eventual use of the center as headquarters for flower shows, art classes, drama groups, musical organizations, craft classes, book reviews and other allied civic activities.

An auditorium seating 200 persons as well as complete kitchen facilities for buffet, garden parties and teas have been included in the plans.

According to Mrs. Arnold MacSpadden, Art Guild president, plans are flexible enough to build portions of the project as funds are available and facilities are required. The building is designed for expansion, including a beautiful walled-in garden for quiet outdoor reading.

Architects for the building are Gamble, Pownall and Gilroy of Ft. Lauderdale. Members of the building committee are Richard Pfeiffer, chairman, F. Gertiser, Mrs. H.D. Gates, Mrs. W.P. Rebout, Mrs. Frank Matthews, W.W. Thomson, with Arnold MacSpadden and Mrs. F. Byron Parks serving as advisors.

Property for the center, donated by Mr. and Mrs. J.M. Schine, overlooks the golf course.

The building will be located in the new million dollar development in the heart of town. The 25-acre tract will include the new Boca Raton Bank, super market, store buildings, as well as the Library and Cultural Center.

Plans are underway for a benefit ball to be held at the Boca Raton Club this season. Proceeds from the ball and the sixth annual art exhibit, to be held this winter, will go to the building fund.

Chamber President Announces Plans For Christmas Lighting Contest

A Christmas lighting contest for the business houses of Boca Raton has been announced by Otto Yark, president of the Boca Raton Chamber of Commerce.

"If effort has any bearing on the end result, the city of Boca Raton will have the best Christmas lighting of any city on the east coast," Yark said. The lighting is divided into two categories, window displays and outdoor lighting. There is a first prize of $15 and a second prize of $10 for each of the categories. A committee of five, headed by Fred Jungbluth, has contacted all business establishments in the city, with over 90 of them agreeing to enter the contest. These entries will display in their windows a hand painted card stating "We're Christmas Lighters."

The outdoor and window lighting, combined with the city's overhead Christmas lighting is expected to put the Boca Raton community in the forefront of those communities that have special Christmas lighting. Judging will be done on the evening of Dec. 9. Awards will be announced through the Chamber of Commerce bulletin.

"We believe," stated Yark, "that the Christmas spirit of a community is greatly enhanced by a tasteful and suitable lighting program. If possible, we intend to make Boca Raton the best lighted town in the State."

Crippled Children's Day

Wednesday, Dec. 7, has been designated as Crippled Children's Day by the Barbers' Union of Palm Beach County. All union barbers will contribute the day receipts for aid to crippled children.

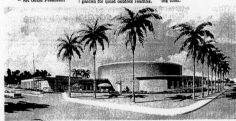

Architect's Drawing of Library and Cultural Art Center

Boca Raton got its first newspaper with the *Boca Raton News* on December 2, 1955. The weekly paper was published by Robert and Lora Britt and had the financial backing of banker Thomas Farrar Fleming and his group of investors. At first, it was published out of the home of editor Margaret Olsson. The first press run was more than 1,200 papers and copies sold for 10 cents. After several decades as a Knight-Ridder newspaper, the *News* was sold in December 1997 to Community Newspaper Holdings, Inc., which in turn sold it to Michael Martin, its former general manager. Attorney Neal Heller and Keiser College president Arthur Keiser bought the paper in 2001. Heller, who runs the paper on a day-to-day basis, has returned the *Boca Raton News* back to what it was: a locally owned newspaper focusing primarily on the community, its people, and events.

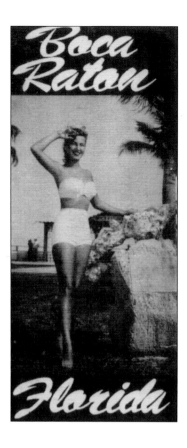

Boca Raton resident Dorothy Steiner won the Miss Florida Pageant in 1953 and was runner-up in the Miss America Pageant.

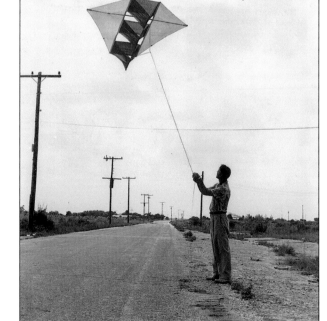

Canadian-born Domina Jalbert moved to Boca Raton in the late 1940s and established an aerology laboratory, where his innovative designs influenced military intelligence-gathering activities, meteorology, aviation, and sports.

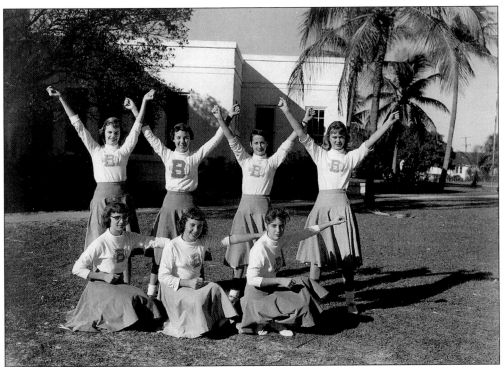

"Give me a B!" The seventh-grade and eighth-grade Bobcats cheerleaders from Boca Raton School demonstrate their spirit.

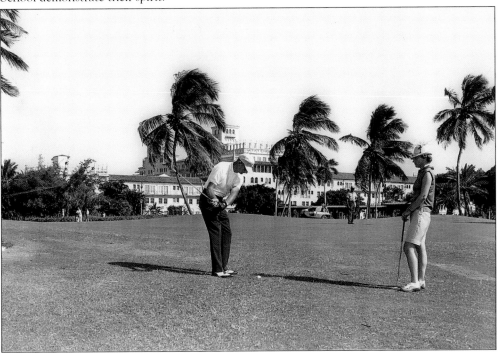

The Boca Raton Resort and Club's golf course has long been recognized as one of Florida's better resort courses. Legend Sam Snead once served as its club pro. (Photograph by Jim Leo.)

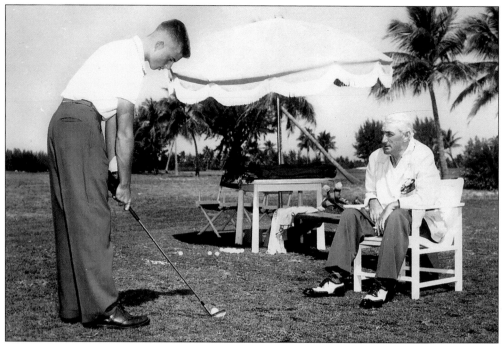

PGA touring pro Tommy Armour takes time to analyze a youngster's swing at the Boca Raton Resort and Club's course. (Photograph by Jim Leo.)

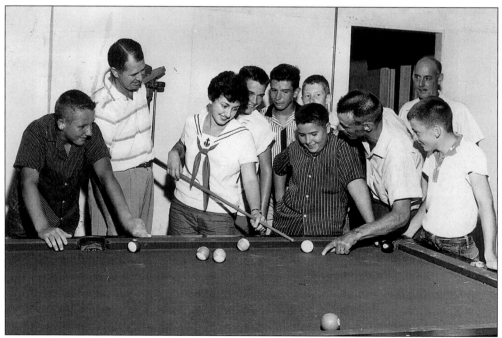

Teen Town, a city-sponsored safe place for preteens and teenagers, was reorganized in 1957 to include more activities. Here, in September 1957, John Hager, Teen Town's supervisor, and chaperones William Prendergast and William Eddinger, look on as Joleen Mucci demonstrates trick shots.

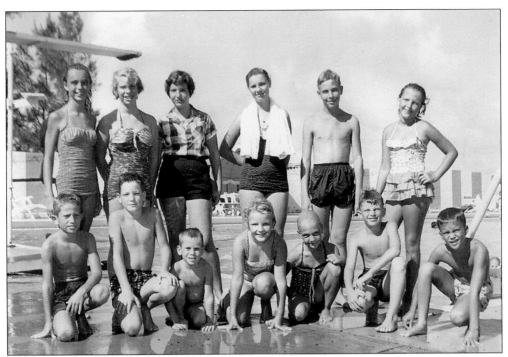

The cabana club was a summertime hotspot, providing swim lessons and a chance to hang out with friends.

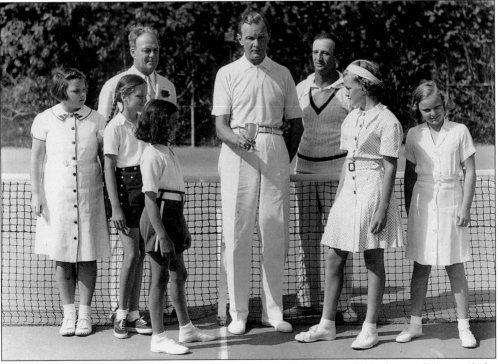

Val Yavorsky, the tennis professional at the Boca Raton Resort and Club, shows off the spoils for tennis tournament competitors.

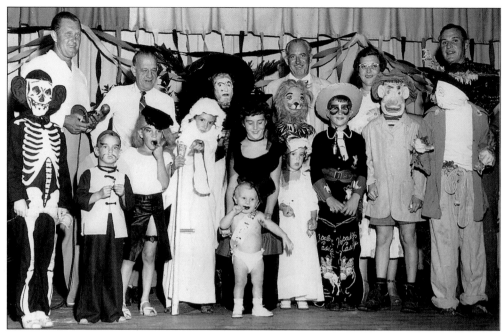

The Boca Raton Hallowe'en Festival was a ghoulishly delightful affair for the youths who attended. Prize winners include Ray Eubank, Bill Eubank, Patty Eddinger, George Seeman Jr., Linda Wright, Chip Douglass, Beatrice Manning, Gail Cortney, Bobby Astras, Wayne Roseke, and George Bieble. In the back row, from left to right, are the judges: Lions Club president Henry Warren, Sidney Pool, Conn C. Curry, Mrs. Ray Shores, and Mayor William O'Donnell.

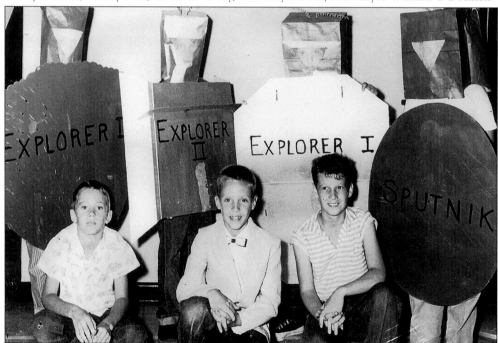

Future space explorers Ray Borchardt, Peter Bondeson, and Warren Christensen show off their interplanetary costumes.

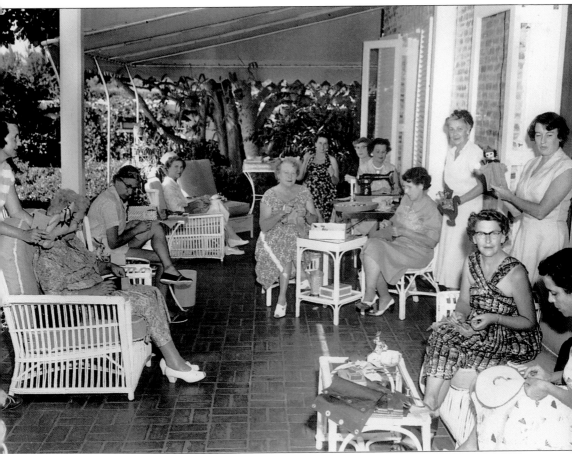

Toy Clinics of America was established in 1951 by Ednah Shapiro. Scouts and other youthful helpers collected used toys; adult volunteers repaired and refurbished the toys and distributed them to hospitalized children. The program blossomed, and Mrs. Shapiro moved its national headquarters to Boca Raton after 1956. The Junior Red Cross joined in, making stuffed toys for children in disaster areas. Here, a group of volunteers work at the Spalsbury home on Spanish River Road. Ednah Shapiro is third from the right; *Palm Beach Post* columnist Georgia Lapham is at the far left, leaning on a chair.

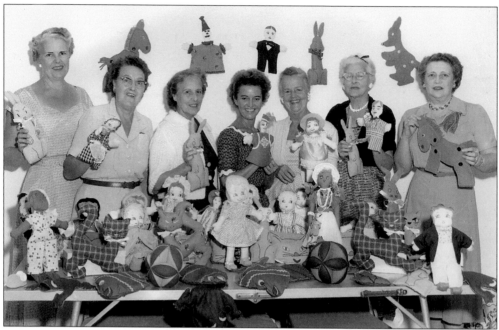

Gladys von Natta (third from left) and Alice Northcutt (third from right) join with friends in displaying toys made at the Toy Clinic.

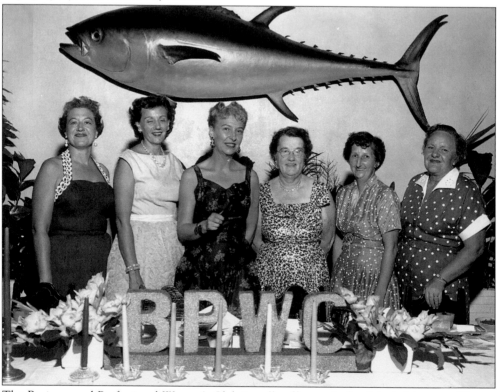

The Business and Professional Women's Club installs officers. At far right is Margaret Olsson, who went on in 1955 to become the first editor of *The Boca Raton News*.

Seven

A PASSION
FOR EDUCATION
1960–1969

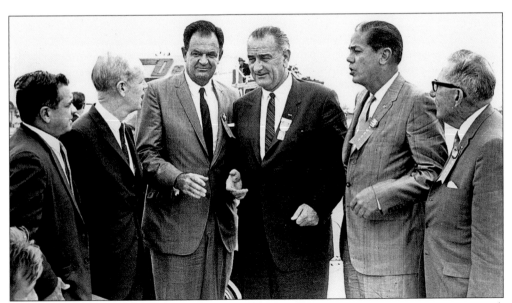

In 1960, the state's fifth publicly supported university, Florida Atlantic University, was created. Ground was broken on December 8, 1962. Banker Thomas F. Fleming, who led the push for the new university, was presented its first Distinguished Service Award at dedication ceremonies in October 1964. The dedication turned out a host of political dignitaries from Tallahassee and Washington. Shown here, from left to right, are Congressman Dante Fascell, Gov. Farris Bryant, Thomas Fleming, President Lyndon B. Johnson, gubernatorial candidate Haydon Burns, and Congressman Claude Pepper. Dr. Kenneth Rast Williams was the university's first president.

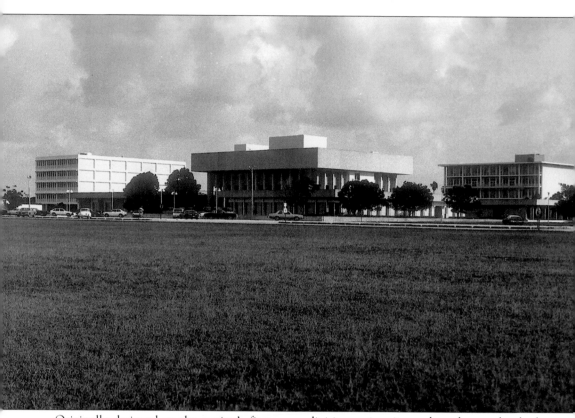

Originally designed as the nation's first upper-division university and graduate school, the college was soon pressured to add traditional features such as dormitories and an intercollegiate athletic program. Underclassmen were admitted for the first time in 1984.

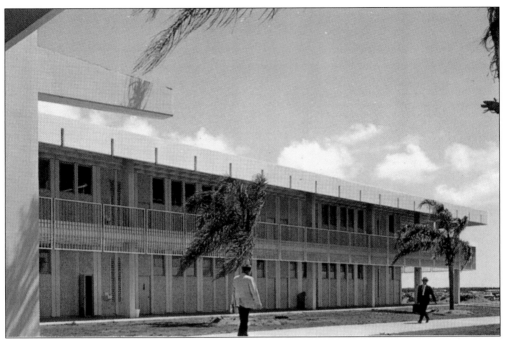

On December 18, 1965, the university's science classroom building was dedicated in the name of Stanton D. Sanson.

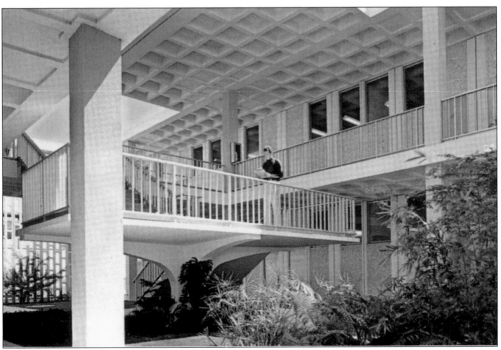

Sanson, who chaired the Florida Council of 100's education committee, had been a forceful advocate for beefing up the state's postsecondary educational system.

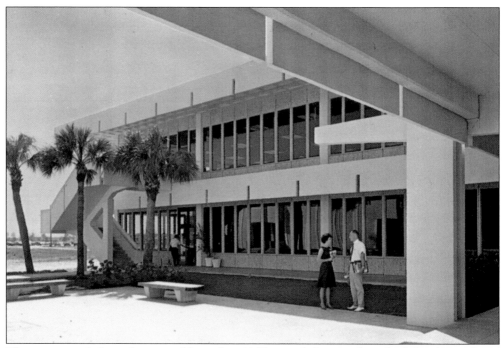

The opening of the cafeteria in November 1965 provided more than food for the students' bodies. It gave them a place not only to grab a bite without having to go off campus, but also to meet friends and pass the time between classes.

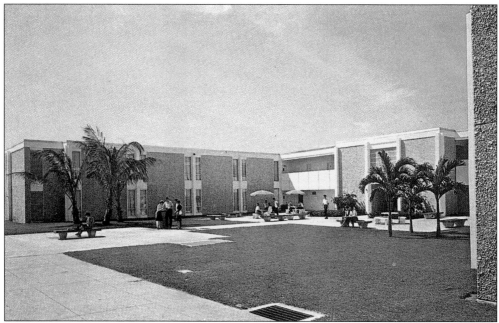

Dormitories were not part of the original plan for Florida Atlantic, but a need for them was recognized almost immediately. Two halls—Algonquin and Modoc—were completed in 1965. Naskapi and Mohave were completed two years later and Seminole and Sekoni two years after that.

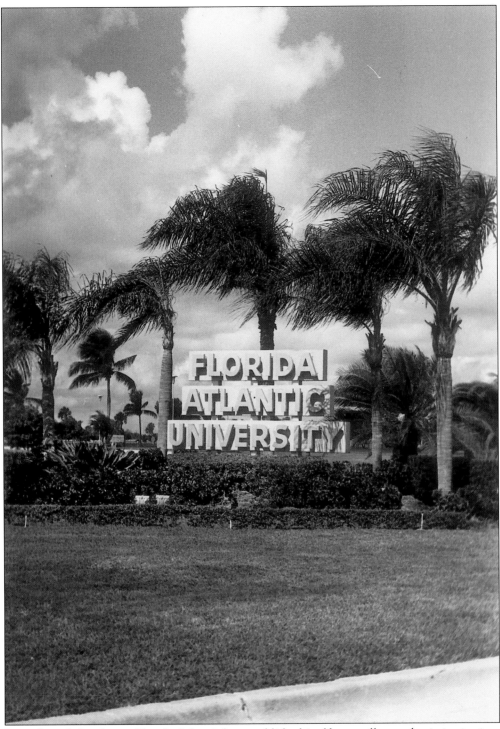

In a relatively brief time, Florida Atlantic has established itself as a stellar academic institution.

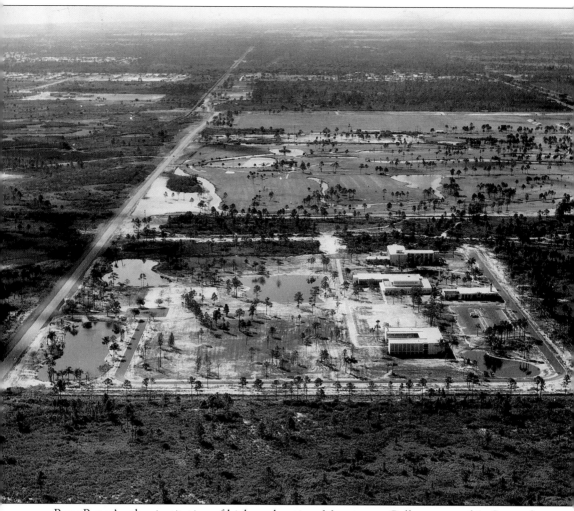

Boca Raton's other institution of higher education, Marymount College, opened in September 1963. A junior college for women, Marymount was situated on a 65-acre campus and was operated by a teaching order, the Religious of the Sacred Heart of Mary. Its first president was Mother Mary Joques. In 1971, Dr. Donald Ross, president of Delaware's Wilmington College, was looking to beef up his library holdings when he visited Marymount. He found the college intriguing, but also struggling to remain viable; it had decided to admit male students. The undeveloped property in the picture's foreground is where Pope John Paul II High School is now located.

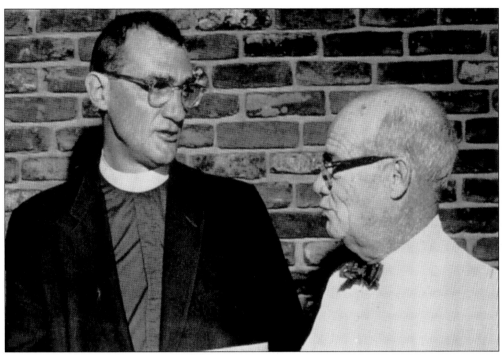

Boca Raton's education boom was hardly confined to postsecondary institutions. In 1961 Rev. Hunter Wyatt-Brown, left, founded St. Andrew's School. Chartered by the Episcopal School Foundation and supported by benefactors such as Alexander, right, and Lucy Henderson, St. Andrew's opened its doors as a boarding school for boys. A companion school for girls, St. Ann's, opened a few years later but failed. After St. Ann's closed, St. Andrew's became coeducational.

Construction quickly got underway on the first Bahamian Colonial buildings on St. Andrew's campus. Originally, chapel services were held in a chickee constructed by Seminole Indians. Once complete, though, St. Andrew's quickly took on the look of a small college. On August 7, 1966, the expansion Miami Dolphins football team opened their first training camp on the school's athletic fields. St. Andrew's offers kindergarten through 12th grade for boys and girls on its 80-acre campus. Day students and boarders are accepted.

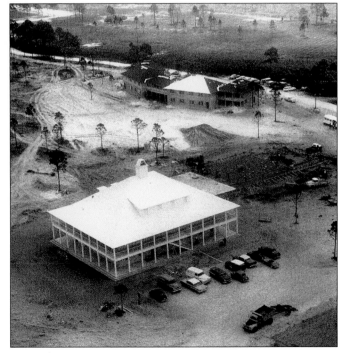

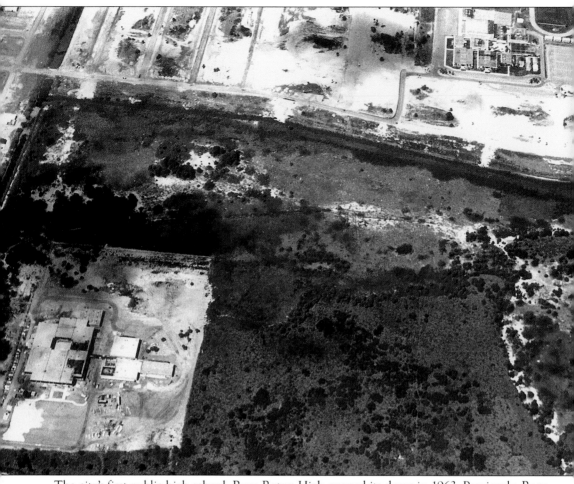

The city's first public high school, Boca Raton High opened its doors in 1963. Previously, Boca Raton–area students traveled by bus daily to Seacrest (now Atlantic) High in Delray Beach. The school was designed by John Shoup and Paul McKinley. Charles Godwin served as its first principal.

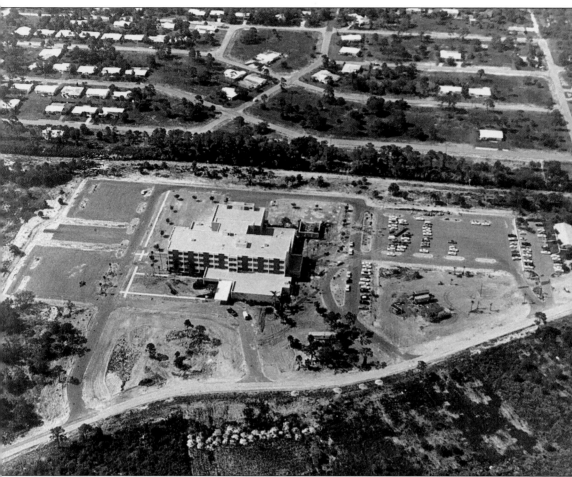

The tragic poisoning deaths of nine-year-old Debbie and three-year-old Randy Drummond in April 1962 proved to city leaders and citizens the need for a hospital within the city. After five years of fund-raisers and the dedicated efforts of community members, four-story, 104-bed Boca Raton Community Hospital opened its doors on July 16, 1967. Because it was built entirely through donations and volunteer support, without tax money, it is sometimes called "The Miracle on Meadows Road."

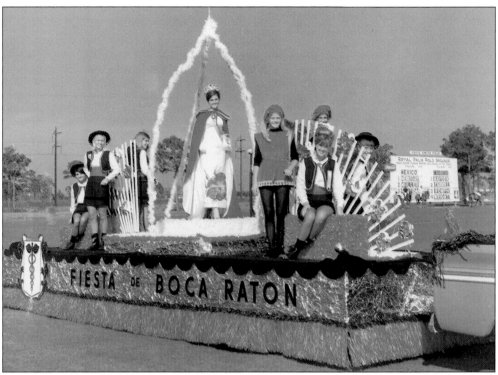

Fiesta de Boca Raton was a town-wide, pre-Lenten celebration that ran from 1964 to 1967. The event featured something for all interests and concluded with the crowning of *la reina de la fiesta*. This picture shows Queen Carol Hutchens and her court at the Royal Palm Polo Club.

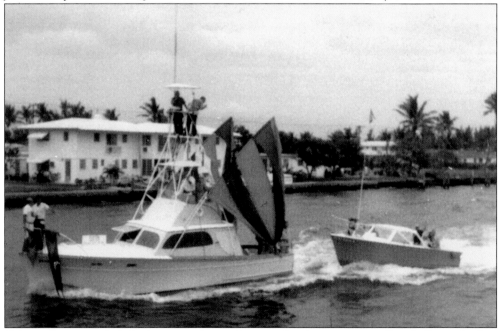

Other activities included a boat parade, art show, and polo games, as well as ballet and other dance exhibitions. The events benefited construction of Boca Raton Community Hospital.

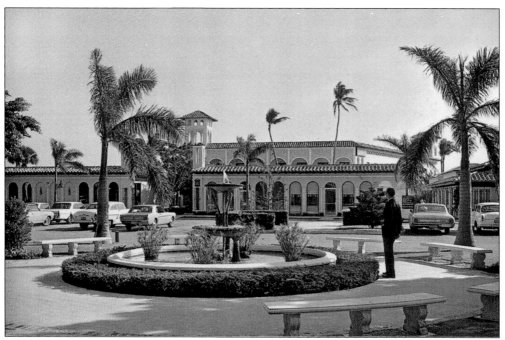

The city's first shopping center, Royal Palm Plaza, opened in 1962.

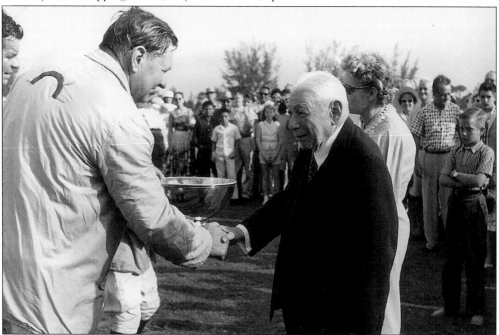

Polo legend Cecil Smith accepts congratulations and a trophy from Arthur Vining Davis at a Royal Palm Polo Club match in 1964. Davis, president of Alcoa, purchased the Boca Raton Hotel and Club in 1956. His company went on to develop thousands of homes in western Boca Raton. Davis also constructed playing fields adjacent to the Boca Raton Hotel and Club. The area where the fields were is now occupied by the Royal Palm Yacht and County Club. Davis later moved the polo club to a 90-acre site on Glades Road. (Photograph by Jim Leo.)

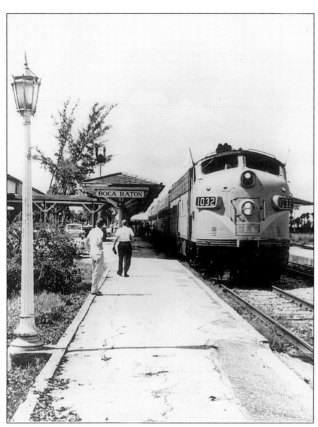

The Florida East Coast Railway, Henry Morrison Flagler's "Railroad to the Sea," ceased passenger travel in 1963.

Citizens listen to speeches by dignitaries at the 1964 dedication ceremonies for City Hall. The building was designed by Victor Rigamont.

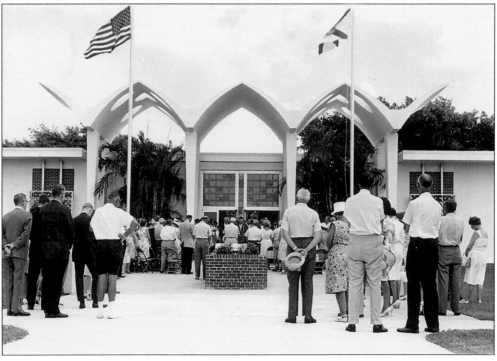

Eight

NEW DIRECTIONS
1970–1979

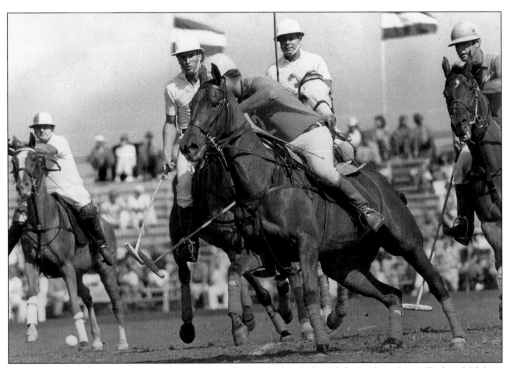

In a 1975 Sunshine League polo match at Royal Palm Polo Club, Milwaukee's Robin Uihlein drives the ball as Chicago's Dick Bunn, John Wigdahl, and Del Carroll give chase. Uihlein's teammate, Joe Barry, backs him up. Oklahoma oilman John T. Oxley took over the club in 1968 and in 1977 built the club's current home on 160 acres along Jog Road. Oxley died in 1996, but sons Tom and Jack continue to keep the polo tradition alive in Boca Raton.

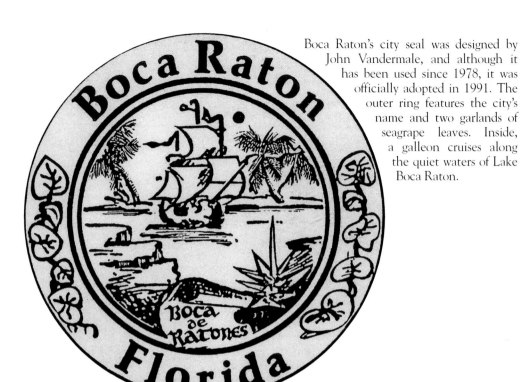

Boca Raton's city seal was designed by John Vandermale, and although it has been used since 1978, it was officially adopted in 1991. The outer ring features the city's name and two garlands of seagrape leaves. Inside, a galleon cruises along the quiet waters of Lake Boca Raton.

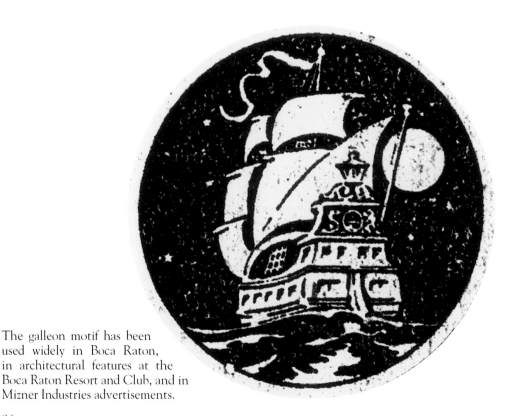

The galleon motif has been used widely in Boca Raton, in architectural features at the Boca Raton Resort and Club, and in Mizner Industries advertisements.

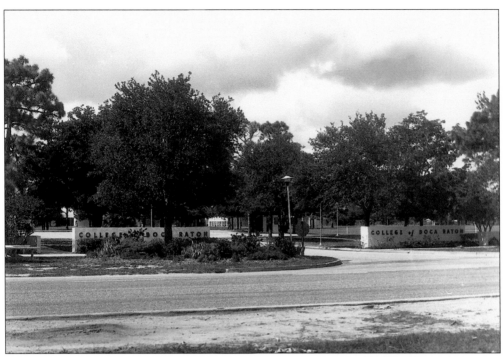

Dr. Donald Ross took the reins at Marymount College, transforming it into a four-year, baccalaureate-granting institution and naming it the College of Boca Raton.

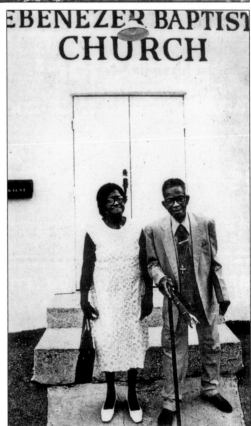

Rev. and Mrs. Henry Clark are the oldest members of Ebenezer Baptist Church in Pearl City.

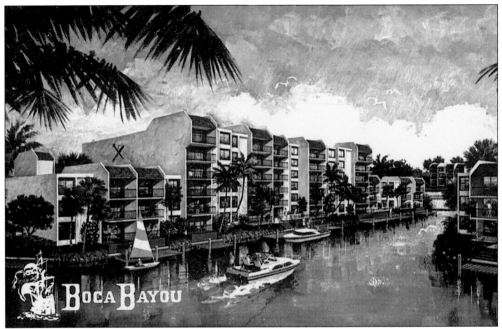

Boca Raton gained popularity as a haven for active retirees. Many preferred to live in condominiums such as Boca Bayou, at the border between Boca Raton and Deerfield Beach. In 1972, an apartment there cost between $19,000 and $42,000.

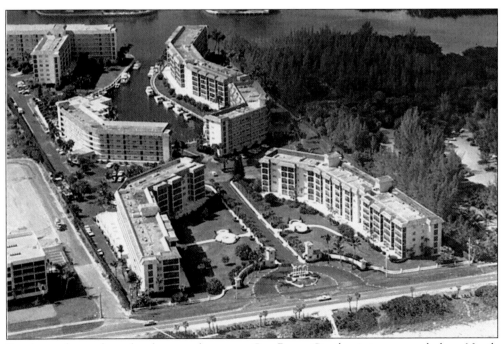

For those who prefer to be closer to the ocean, San Remo Condominiums sprawl along North Ocean Boulevard, adjacent to the south boundary of Spanish River Park.

Nine

FAITH, HOPE, AND CHARITY 1980–1989

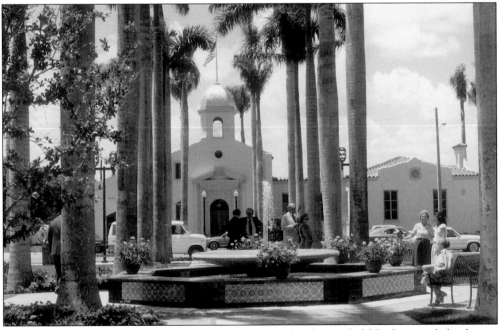

The Boca Raton City Council opened the decade with a brave, bold look toward the future. They created the Community Redevelopment Agency to pump life back into the downtown area. The agency's first project was to revitalize Sanborn Square on Federal Highway, across the street from Town Hall. In 1982, the city leased Town Hall to the Boca Raton Historical Society for restoration purposes. Through grants and private fund-raising the building was restored and is listed on the National Register of Historic Places. (Photograph by Sanford Smith.)

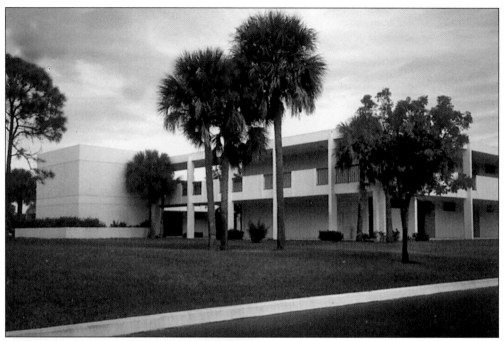

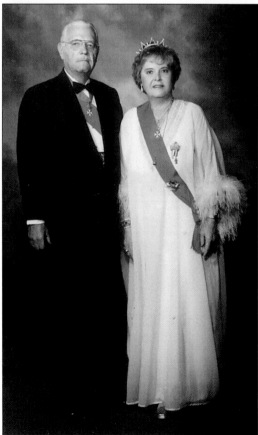

When Pope John Paul II High School opened on August 25, 1980, Catholic students rejoiced. No longer would they have to travel to Cardinal Newman in West Palm Beach or to Cardinal Gibbons in Fort Lauderdale. Carmelite Brother Michael Welch was the founding principal of the school, the first in the nation to be named after the pontiff, who became pope in October 1978.

Adolph and Henrietta de Hoernle first visited Boca Raton in the late 1970s, after Adolph de Hoernle had sold his company in Yonkers, New York, and moved to Palm Beach. In 1981, the year they were created count and countess, they became permanent residents. Count de Hoernle died in 1996, but the countess continues their tradition of supporting worthwhile endeavors in the community, such as the YMCA, Lynn University, Florida Atlantic University, the Junior League of Boca Raton, Palm Beach Community College, Boca Raton Community Hospital, the Boca Raton Historical Society, and many more.

In August 1981, IBM, which had been in Boca Raton since 1966, debuted a personal computer that revolutionized the American office. Sales of the IBM PC exceeded $4.5 billion.

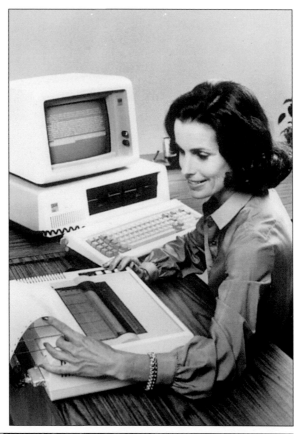

At the time of the IBM PC's release, the work force at the company's 300,000-square-foot complex had swollen to nearly 10,000. But the gravy train did not last much longer. In June 1985, 200 executives were transferred to a plant in New Jersey. In the summer of 1988, 1,600 workers were released and production at the Boca Raton plant was curtailed.

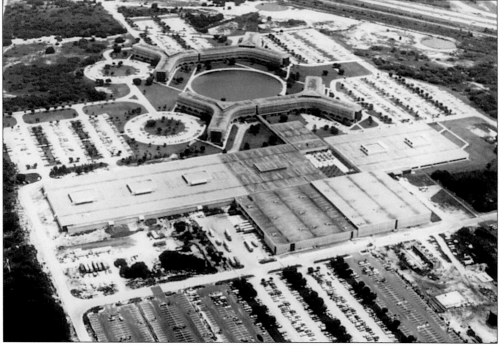

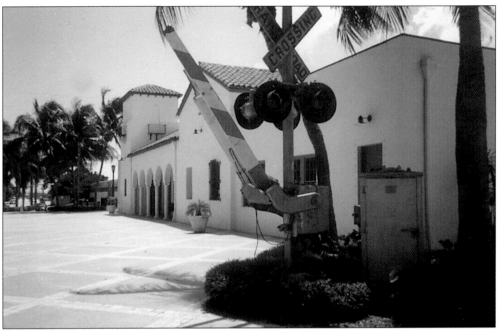

The Boca Raton Historical Society purchased and restored the historic FEC passenger railway station. Donations by the Count and Countess de Hoernle significantly financed the restoration, and the station is named the Count de Hoernle Pavilion in his honor. The station is listed on the National Register of Historic Places.

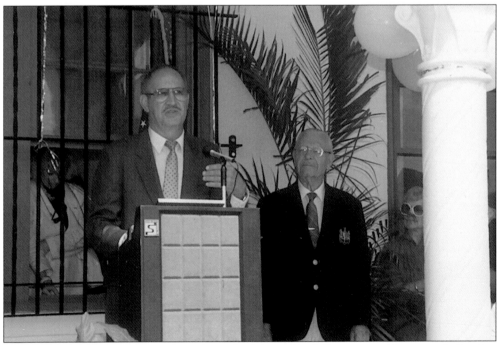

With Count Adolph de Hoernle at his side, Mayor Emil Danciu presides over dedication ceremonies for the FEC passenger railway station.

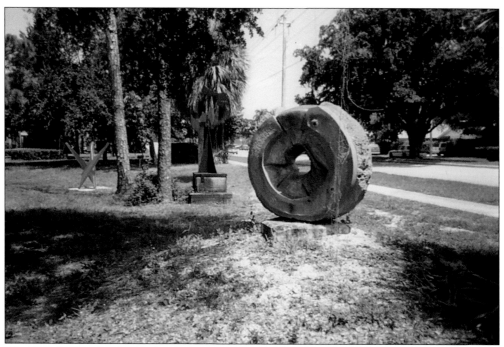

The Boca Raton Art Guild changed its name to the Boca Raton Museum of Art in 1985. At the organization's studios on Palmetto Park Road, modern sculptures use the old concrete basis from Addison Mizner's radio station as pedestals.

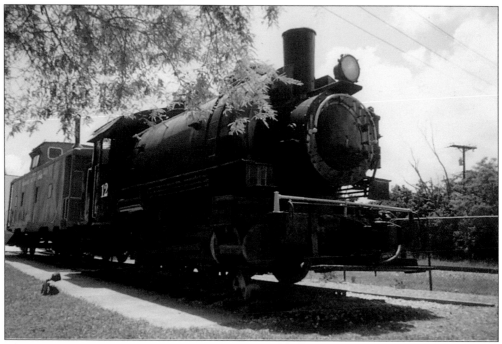

The Boca Raton Historical Society received an Outstanding Achievement Award for the restoration of the train station, presented by the Florida Trust for Historic Preservation. The engine and Atlantic Coast Line caboose there prove to be a huge hit with children.

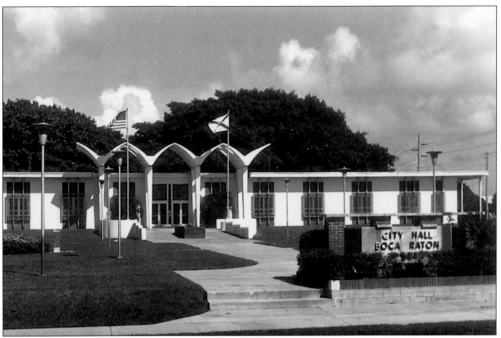

City Hall's expansion and remodeling retains many elements of the original Victor Rigamont design into the refurbished building.

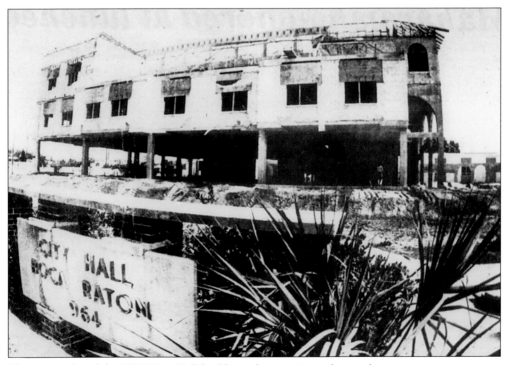

The remainder of the 1964 City Hall building after gutting is shown above.

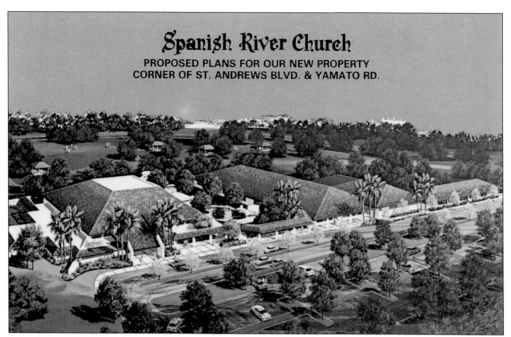

Spanish River Church

PROPOSED PLANS FOR OUR NEW PROPERTY
CORNER OF ST. ANDREWS BLVD. & YAMATO RD.

The Spanish River Church got its start in temporary quarters in March 1967 and experienced phenomenal growth. It dedicated its current home at the corner of Yamato Road and St. Andrew's Boulevard on November 3, 1985. Spread out over the 20 acres of church property today is a 400-seat chapel, 1,200-seat worship center, a school for children in pre-school to eighth grade, a counseling center, café, youth-education center, seminary, and a degree-granting Christian ministries center.

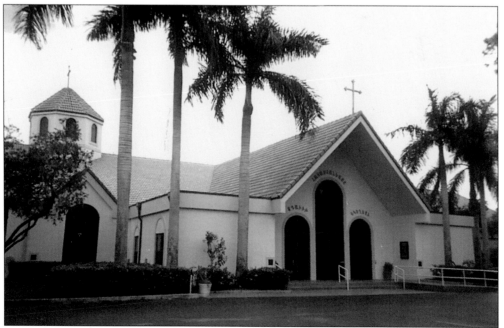

St. David Armenian Church, like Spanish River Church, is situated on the strip of Yamato Road known as Church Row.

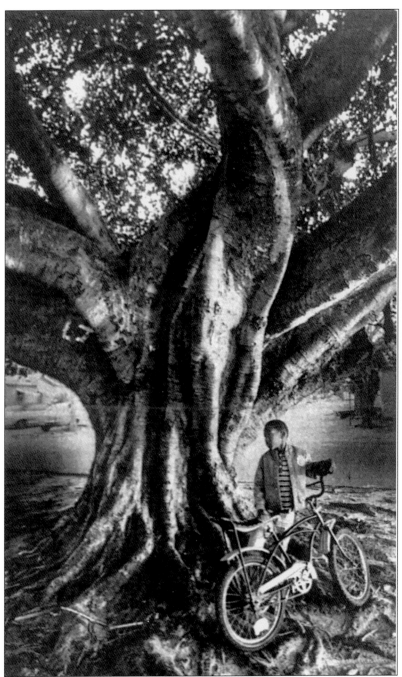

An era ended when a well-loved banyan tree called "the tree of learning" was cut down. The tree was planted in 1933 by J.C. Mitchell and his sons near the Mitchell Arcade at the corner of Dixie and Palmetto Park Road. Deals—legal and otherwise—were consummated beneath its canopy of limbs. Children played under the tree and lovers carved their initials into the bark. It was both a meeting place and a landmark. When Dixie Highway was to be widened, the tree either had to be moved or had to go. The cost of moving it was prohibitive, so workers cut it down in 1987.

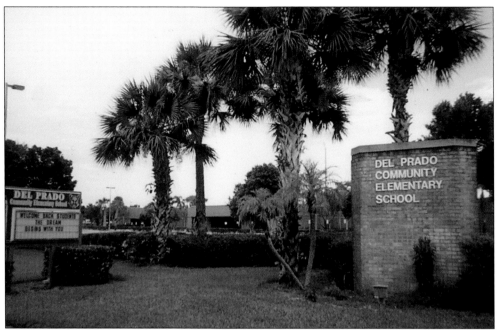

Del Prado Elementary School is representative of the elementary schools in the area. It opened in 1989 and has won a variety of state and national awards including the Florida Little Red Schoolhouse Award and the Golden School Award. In each of the five years Del Prado has received a rating based on the Florida Comprehensive Academic Testing program, the school has not scored below an A.

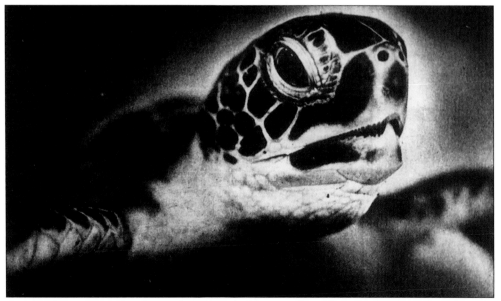

Among the most sought-after and pampered visitors to Boca Raton's shore are the sea turtles who lay their eggs in the sand at high tide. Visitors often come at night to watch the hatchlings crawl from the sand and into the surf. Lights tend to distract them, and the stretch of beach along Spanish River Park has been equipped with special lights to avoid disorienting the turtles. This turtle was released to the sea in 1981.

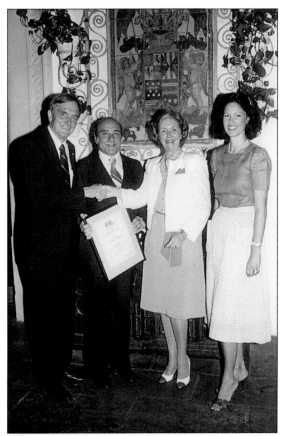

In ceremonies at the Boca Raton Hotel and Club in May 1981, the Florida Historic Trust presented an award to Rhea Chiles for promoting Florida House in Washington, D.C. From left to right are her husband, Sen. Lawton Chiles, Secretary of State George Firestone, Rhea Chiles, and Mrs. David Dickinson.

Palm Beach Community College began adding satellite centers to increase its reach from its main campus in Lake Worth. The satellite centers were begun in Boca Raton, Belle Glade, and Palm Beach Gardens in the early 1970s. Between 1974 and 1989, the centers underwent accelerated development. The Boca Raton center, on the northern part of Florida Atlantic's campus, serves as the college's technology campus and offers a comprehensive variety of programs.

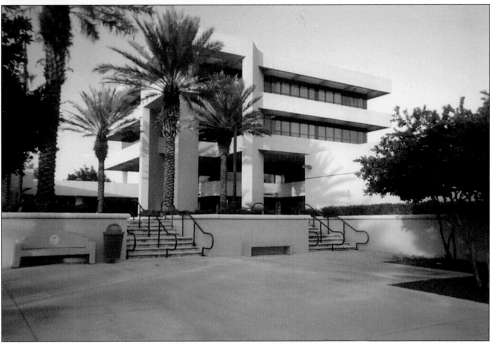

Ten

FAST FORWARD
1990–1999

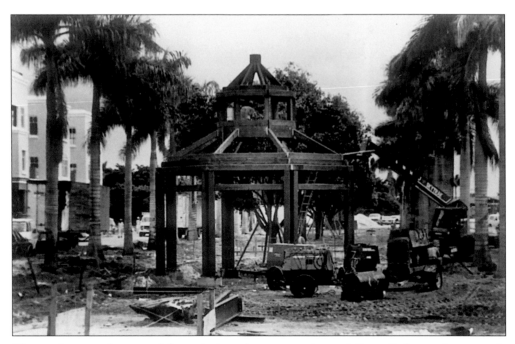

The gazebo near the central fountain is under construction at Mizner Park, a unique upscale shopping, dining, residential/office, and cultural arts center on the site of the Boca Raton Mall.

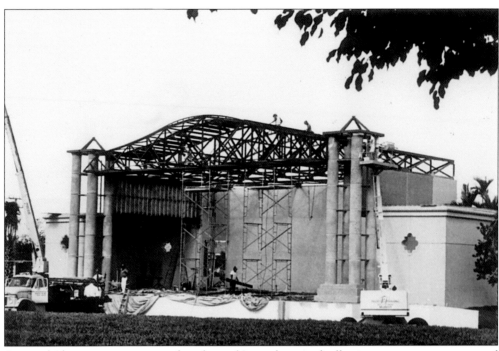

An amphitheater was constructed at the park's northern end, allowing concert-goers to spread out a blanket or bring a folding chair and enjoy music or theater under the sun or the stars.

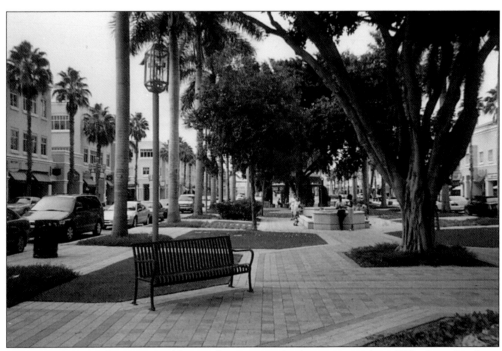

Mizner Park opened in 1991 and has undergone steady change since then. Whether it's taking in a film, visiting the museum, shopping, eating at one of the many restaurants, or just enjoying a leisurely stroll, Mizner Park offers a safe, serene environment.

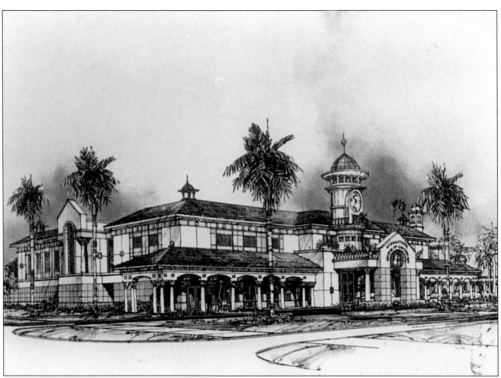

The International Museum of
Cartoon Art, a collection of
more than 160,000 cartoons
of all sorts and 10,000 books
on the cartoonist's art,
opened in Mizner Park in
1992. The museum had
gotten its start in Greenwich,
Connecticut, then moved to
Rye Brook, New York, before
relocating in Boca Raton.

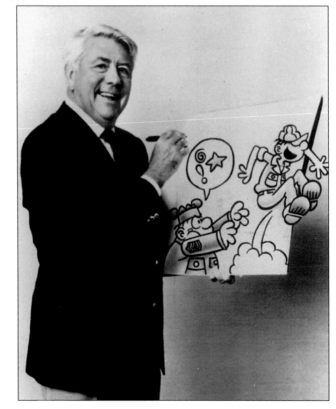

Mort Walker, creator of "Beetle
Bailey," was the visionary
behind the International
Museum of Cartoon Art.

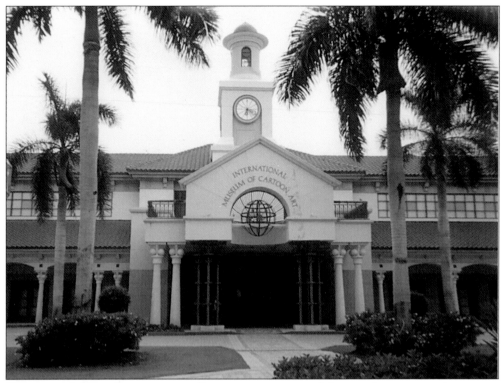

The museum's $10 million cartoon collection never generated the crowds or community support its creators had envisioned. It closed on July 31, 2002.

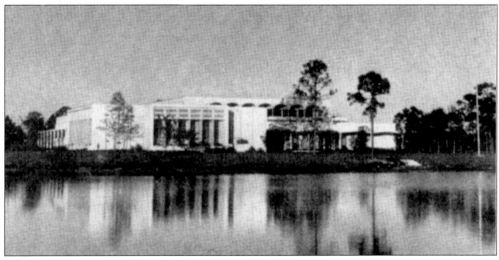

In 1991, the College of Boca Raton changed its name to Lynn University, indicating its change to university status and honoring benefactors Eugene and Christine Lynn.

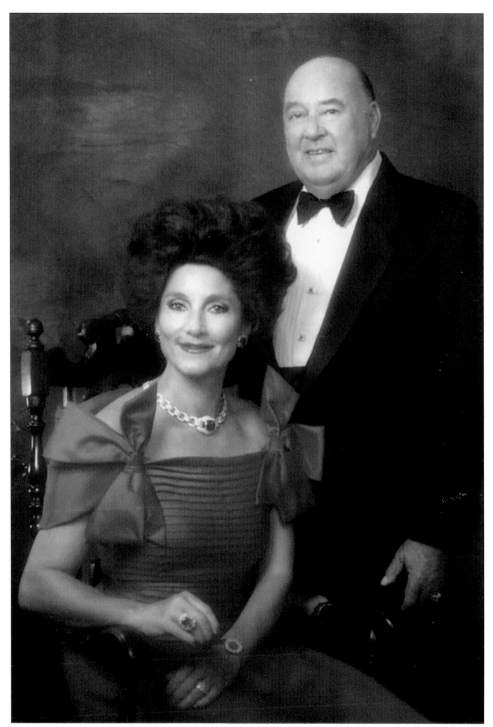

Lynn, an insurance executive, and his Norwegian-born wife, a nurse, supported a variety of causes but particularly education and healthcare. In addition to their gifts to Lynn University, they also were generous benefactors to Florida Atlantic University. Eugene Lynn died on November 28, 1999, but Christine Lynn remains active in social and philanthropic circles.

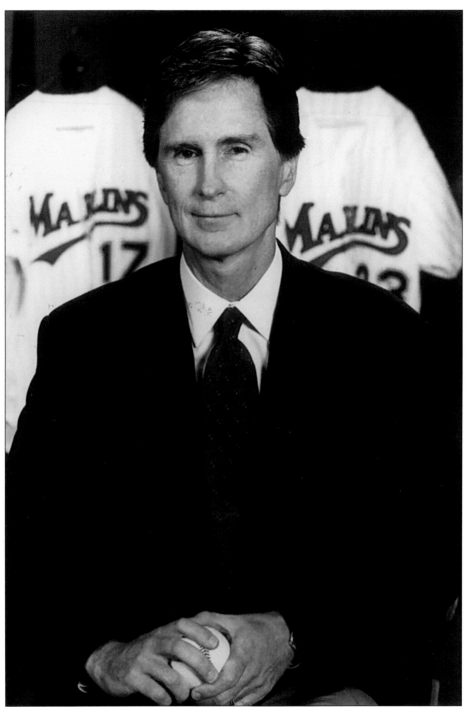

In 1998, futures trader, philanthropist, and Boca Raton resident John Henry lived out the ultimate fan fantasy as he purchased the 1997 World Series champion Florida Marlins for $150 million. On February 11, 2002, he sold the team to Montreal Expos owner Jeffrey Loria for $158.5 million. Sixteen days later, the team of Henry, Tom Werner, and Larry Lucchino became owners of the Boston Red Sox.

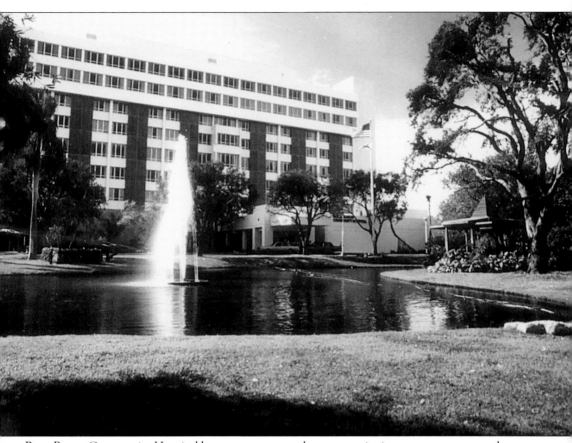

Boca Raton Community Hospital has grown to serve the community in many ways, among them adding an imaging center and outpatient surgical department in 1986 and the Lynn Regional Cancer Center and One Family Place, a maternity and child care center, in 1992.

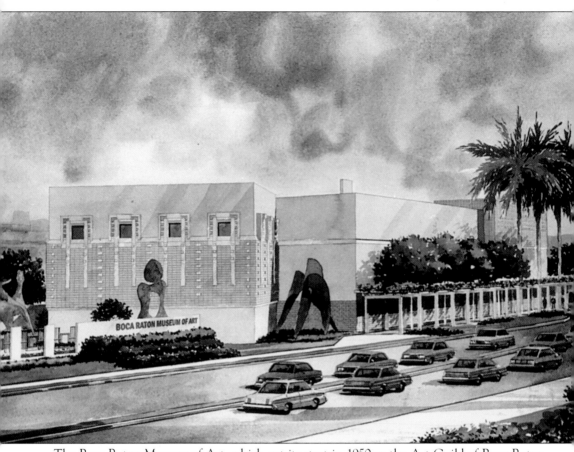

The Boca Raton Museum of Art, which got its start in 1950 as the Art Guild of Boca Raton, opened the doors to a 44,000-square-foot facility in Mizner Park on January 24, 2001.

Eleven

THE NEW MILLENNIUM AND BEYOND

Its reputation as an academic institution already ensured, Florida Atlantic University moved into the upper echelon of college athletics with the addition of a football program. Howard Schnellenberger, who led the University of Miami to an NCAA football title, was hired to build the program, then to become its first head coach. Coach Schnellenberger is shown on the sidelines of the Owls' first game, against Slippery Rock University on September 4, 2001. (Photo by J.C. Ridley.)

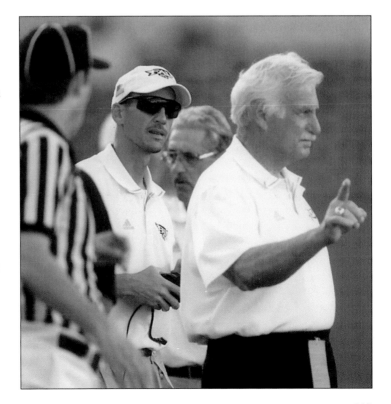

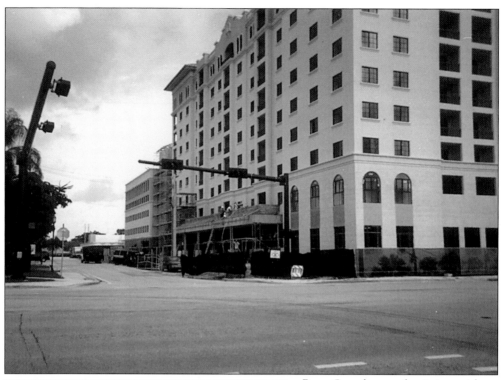

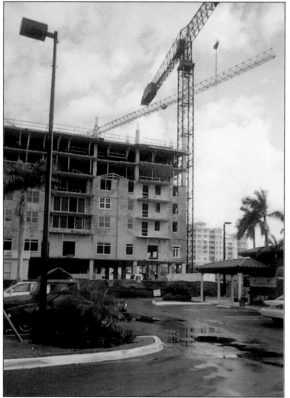

Boca Grand, a condominium with retail shops and businesses at the ground level, rises on the downtown space formerly occupied by *The Boca Raton News.*

Among other downtown construction during the start of the 21st century was Royal Palm Place, which broke ground in mid-June 2002. The project will transform Royal Palm Plaza from a sprawling center of shops and restaurants to a nine-story building with one floor of retail space, one floor of offices, and the remainder, apartments.

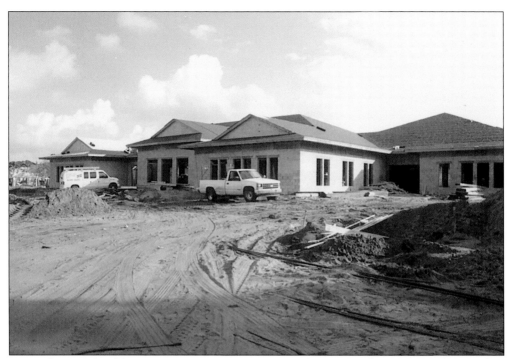

St. Andrew's School has been in an expansion mode. This picture shows work in progress on the Lower School, which was dedicated in 2000. About 1,000 students attend the school in grades kindergarten through twelfth.

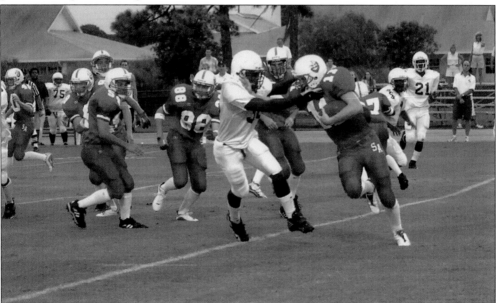

Athletic facilities at St. Andrew's have been improved, too. In this picture, a Scots running back tries to break free of the grasp of a Broward Christian School tackler at Don Jones Field, named for the school's beloved athetic director and head coach from 1980 to 1985 who died suddenly of a heart attack. St. Andrew's athletic fields were used for the film *Paper Lion*, filmed during the winter of 1967–1968. (Photo by Cindy Newnam.)

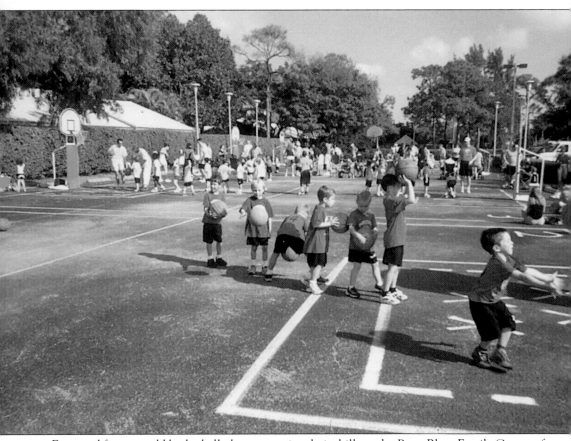

Four- and five-year-old basketball players practice their skills at the Peter Blum Family Center of the YMCA of South Palm Beach County. Led by furniture company owner Peter Blum, his wife Teena, and a host of area philanthropists, the Boca Raton YMCA embarked on an aggressive $7 million, 37,000-square-foot expansion begun in September 2003 with anticipated completion in 2005. Plans for the expansion call for a variety of enhancements, among them a gymnasium, a second enclosed swimming pool, and enhanced playgrounds. The Boca Raton YMCA was founded in 1972 with about 200 members and a loaned facility. It opened its Palmetto Circle South headquarters in 1975 and serves about 25,000 people annually.

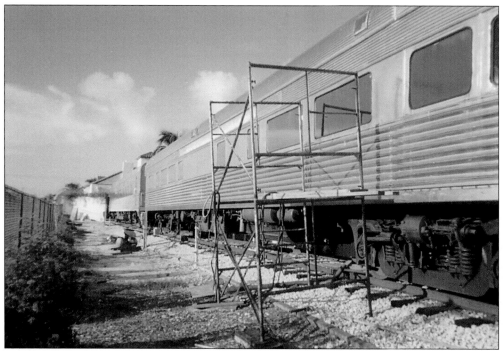

Work commenced in 2001 on the effort of the Boca Raton Historical Society to restore a Seaboard Air Line dining car and a lounge car, which have both already been placed on the National Register of Historic Places. Both cars were built in 1947.

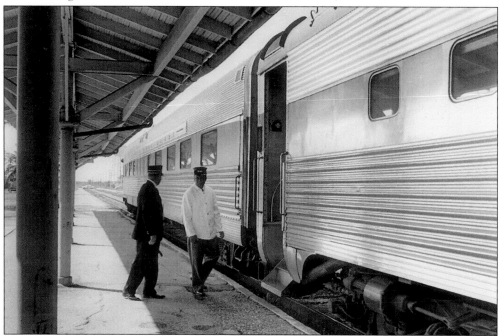

A sleekly designed streamliner pulls into the Boca Raton FEC station in the early 1960s. They were a common sight on the American rails from the mid-1930s through the 1970s. (Photo by Jack Hutton, *Boca Raton News*.)

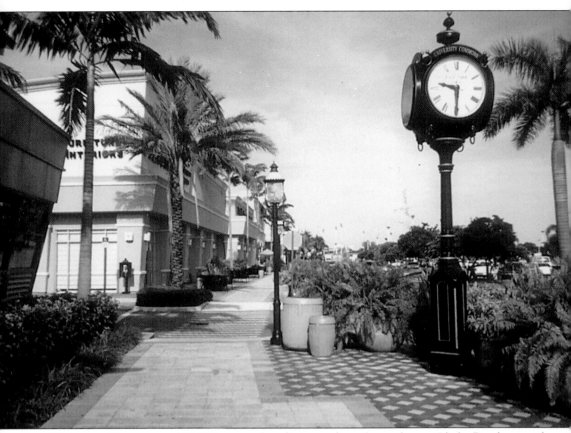

University Commons, a 169,709-square-foot dining and retail complex on Glades Road, opened in 2001. The center features stores such as Barnes & Noble, Whole Foods Market, and Circuit City and restaurants such as P.F. Chang's, China Bistro, and J. Alexander's. The center is built on property owned by Florida Atlantic University.

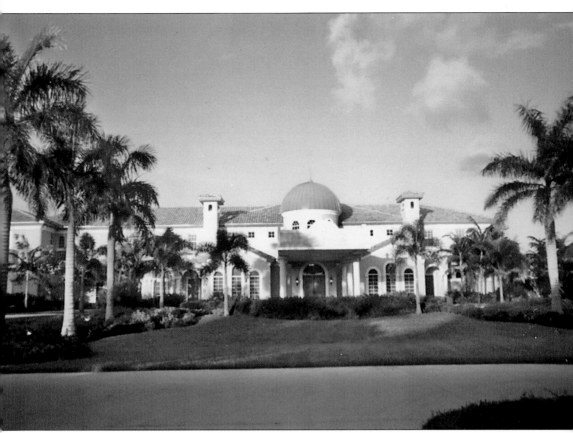

The 14,000-square-foot Eleanor R. Baldwin House, dedicated on June 6, 2002, serves as the official residence of Florida Atlantic University's president and as a reception center for the university. The $2 million building is named for the Boca Raton philanthropist, who spent 34 years as a secondary school teacher in Broward County.

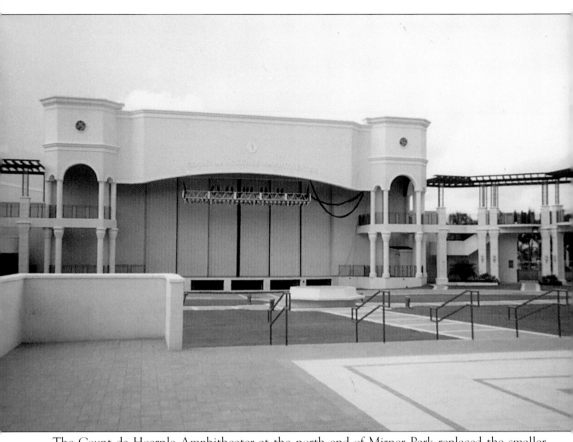

The Count de Hoernle Amphitheater at the north end of Mizner Park replaced the smaller amphitheater and provides a gracious home for public events in the park as well as allowing greater numbers of people to attend these popular events.

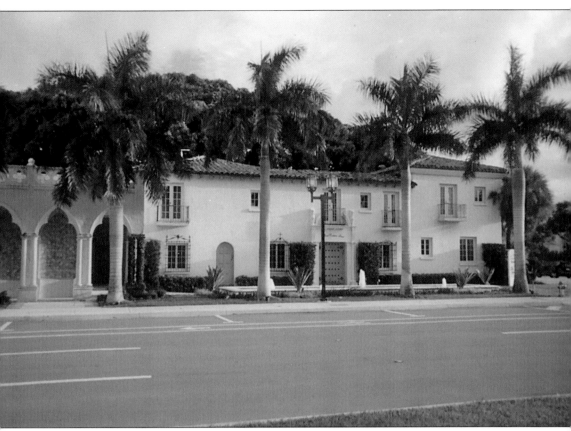

In 1927, after the land boom went bust and Addison Mizner fled back to Palm Beach and the Mizner Development Corporation's headquarters were vacant, Judge Willis Brown proposed transforming the administration building into Boy City, "the only school in America of actual citizenship," designed for boys 12 to 18 years of age. Though Mizner left the area, his influence on architecture has remained and the Mizner name lives on in an elementary school, a shopping center/cultural complex, and many businesses. The administrative offices have since been transformed into a restaurant.

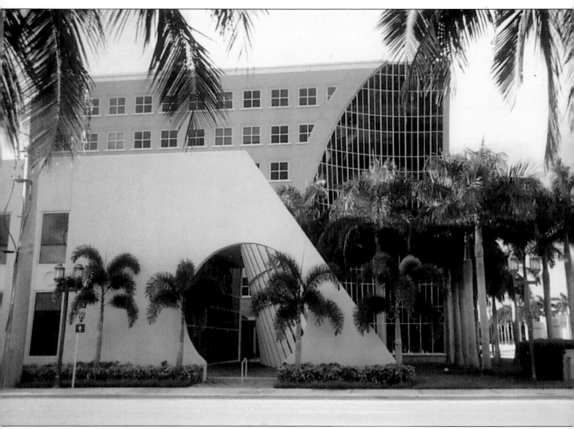

Although much of Boca Raton's architecture harkens back to the Mizner era, some of the city's newer buildings, such as the Wachovia Bank building, break the mold, providing fresh, innovative designs.

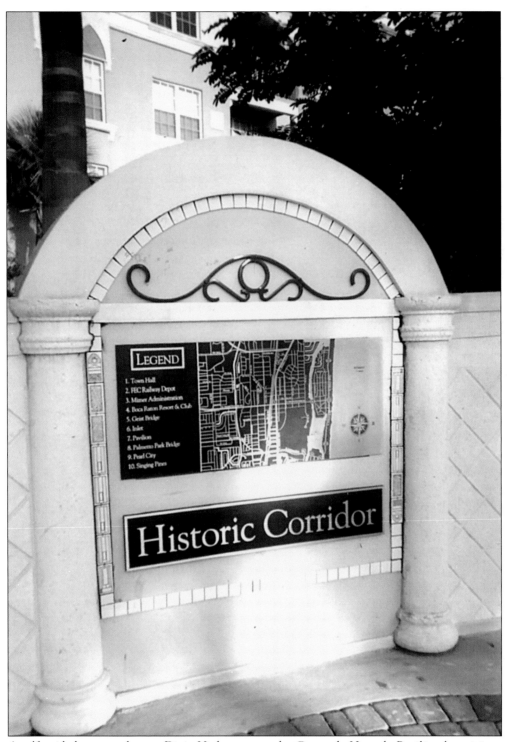

LEGEND
1. Town Hall
2. FEC Railway Depot
3. Mizner Administration
4. Boca Raton Resort & Club
5. Geist Bridge
6. Inlet
7. Pavilion
8. Palmetto Park Bridge
9. Pearl City
10. Singing Pines

Historic Corridor

A self-guided tour marker on Dixie Highway near the Count de Hoernle Pavilion lets visitors explore the city's architectural and historical treasures at their own pace. A tour of the sites makes for a delightful stroll.

SOURCES

"Addison Mizner's Ritz-Carlton Cloister Opens," *The Spanish River Papers*, Fall 1982.

Ashton, Jacqueline. *Boca Raton Pioneers and Addison Mizner*. Boca Raton: Jacqueline Ashton Waldeck, 1984.

Austin, Daniel F. and David M. McJunkin. "The Legend of Boca Ratones," *The Spanish River Papers*, May 1981.

Curl, Donald W. and John P. Johnson. *Boca Raton: A Pictorial History*. Virginia Beach: The Donning Company, 1990.

———*Florida Atlantic University*. Charleston, SC: Arcadia Publishing, 2000.

Evans, Arthur S., Jr. and David Lee. *Pearl City, Florida: A Black Community Remembers*. Boca Raton: Florida Atlantic University Press, 1990.

Johnson, Stanley, and Phyllis Shapiro. *Once Upon a Time: The Story of Boca Raton*. Boca Raton: The Arvida Corporation, 1987.

Kinney, Henry. *Once Upon a Time: The Legend of the Boca Raton Hotel & Club*. Boca Raton: The Arvida Corporation, 1966.

Konrad, Irene. *Farewell Africa, U.S.A. Hail Camino Gardens*. Boca Raton: Camino Gardens Association, 2000.

Mizner, Addison. *The Many Mizners*. New York: Sears Publishing Co. Inc., 1932.

Murphy, Stephanie and Cynthia Thuma. *The Insiders' Guide to Boca Raton and the Palm Beaches*. Manteo, NC: The Insiders' Guides, Inc., 1995.

Posey, William M., *A History of St. Andrew's School: The First Thirty Years (1962–1992)*. Boca Raton: St. Andrew's School.

Simon, Sandy. *Remembering: A History of Florida's South Palm Beach County 1894-1998*. Delray Beach, FL.: The Cedars Group, 1999.

"The Mizner Development Corporation's Administration Buildings," *The Spanish River Papers*, Fall/Winter 1983/84.

Vickers, Raymond B. *Panic in Paradise: Florida's Banking Crash of 1926*. Tuscaloosa, AL.: University of Alabama Press, 1994.

Waldeck, Jackie Ashton. *Boca Raton: A Romance of the Past*. Boca Raton: The Bicentennial Committee of Boca Raton, 1981.

"YMCA to break ground on $7 million expansion," *Boca Raton News*, August 27, 2003, page 6.